Excel 97

═fast & easy

How to Order:

For information on quantity discounts contact the publisher: Prima Publishing, P.O. Box 1260BK, Rocklin, CA 95677-1260; (916) 632-4400. On your letterhead include information concerning the intended use of the books and the number of books you wish to purchase. For individual orders, turn to the back of this book for more information.

Excel 97

fast & easy

Nancy Stevenson

PRIMA PUBLISHING

To Norma and Steve

Acquisitions Manager: Alan Harris
Managing Editor: Tad Ringo
Product Marketing Specialist: Julie Barton

Acquisitions Editor: Jenny L.Watson
Assistant Acquisitions Editor: Christy Clinton
Development Editors: Kelli Crump, Suzanne Weixel
Project Editor: Kelli Crump
Editorial Coordinator: Stacie Drudge
Technical Reviewers: Suzanne Weixel, David Maguiness, Ray Link
Interior Design and Layout: Marian Hartsough
Cover Design: Vanessa Perez
Indexer: Emily Glossbrenner

ISBN: 0-7615-1008-7
Library of Congress Catalog Card Number: 96-72132
Printed in the United States of America

97 98 99 HH 10 9 8 7 6 5 4 3

Acknowledgments

Many thanks to the folks at Prima who continue to have faith in my abilities: Jenny Watson, the Acquisitions Editor who gave me the work and a shoulder to cry on; Tad Ringo, their very capable Managing Editor; and Kelli Crump for her able project management and for going the extra mile on this one. My sincere thanks go to Barb Terry, a friend and great author, who stepped in at the eleventh hour and contributed significant material to the book. Thanks also go to Suzanne Weixel for her often helpful editorial insight.

And as always, to Graham for giving me the space to write and carry on.

About the Author

Nancy Stevenson is an author specializing in technology and how-to books. With over a dozen books to her credit, she has also authored articles for national magazines and a mystery novel (in her upper left-hand drawer; yet to be published). In the past, Nancy has also been a software trainer/consultant, video producer, and an instructor of technical writing at the university level.

Contents at a Glance

Contents

PART II
CONSTRUCTING LARGER WORKSHEETS 37

PART IV
CREATING CHARTS
AND MAPS OF YOUR DATA 193

Introduction

This new Visual Learning Guide from Prima Publishing will help you open up the power of Microsoft Excel, the world's best-selling worksheet program. Worksheet—or spreadsheet—software is designed to organize numerical data into rows and columns on your computer screen. These types of programs have revolutionized the way that we work with numbers, and have made even the most complex and challenging computations accessible to everyday people like you.

The problem with many worksheet programs is that new users can easily get lost in a maze of grids and formulas, and the result of a day of hard work usually ends up being a high level of frustration. Visual Learning Guides teach you with a step-by-step approach, clear language, and color illustrations of exactly what you will see on your screen. The *Excel 97 Visual Learning Guide* provides the tools you need to successfully tackle the potentially overwhelming challenge of learning to use Excel 97. You will be able to quickly tap into the program's user-friendly design and powerful worksheet calculating ability.

WHO SHOULD READ THIS BOOK?

The easy-to-follow, highly visual nature of this book makes it the perfect learning tool for a beginning computer user. However, it is also ideal for those who are new to this version of Excel, or those who feel comfortable with computers and software, but have never used a spreadsheet program before.

In addition, anyone using a software application always needs an occasional reminder about the steps required to perform a particular task. By using the *Excel 97*

Visual Learning Guide, any level of user can look up steps for a task quickly without having to plow through pages of descriptions. In short, this book can be used by the beginning-to-intermediate computer user as a learning tool or as a step-by-step task reference.

ADDED ADVICE TO MAKE YOU A PRO

You'll notice that this book uses steps and keeps explanations to a minimum to help you learn faster. Included in the book are a few elements that provide some additional comments to help you master the program, without encumbering your progress through the steps:

✦ **Tips** often offer shortcuts when performing an action, or a hint about a feature that might make your work in Excel quicker and easier.

✦ **Notes** give you a bit of background or additional information about a feature, or advice about how to use the feature in your day-to-day activities.

In addition, a helpful appendix will take you through one of Excel's most useful templates to create your own customized expense statement. When you finish, you can begin using this template in your work right away!

Read and enjoy this Visual Learning Guide. It is certainly the fastest and easiest way to learn Microsoft Excel 97!

PART I

Building Your First Worksheet

1 Welcome to Excel 97

Excel is a replacement for the accountant's columnar pad, sharp pencil, and calculator. However, you don't have to be an accountant to benefit from Excel. If you have complex calculations to figure out, Excel can handle them with ease. Yet even if your calculations are simple, Excel will make working with numbers fun and easy. The great thing about Excel is that you can present your data so that it has impact. You can create colorful charts, print transparencies or hard copy reports, add clip art and your company logo, and more! In this chapter, you'll learn how to:

✦ Start Excel 97

✦ Enter text and numbers

✦ Enter a simple formula

✦ Play what if?

✦ Close a worksheet

STARTING EXCEL 97

The Windows Start button is the easiest way to find your programs.

1. **Click** on the **Start button** on the Taskbar with the left mouse button. A pop-up menu will appear.

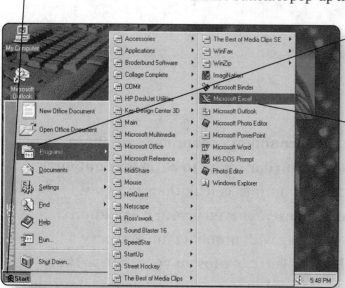

2. Move the **mouse arrow** up the menu to **Programs** to highlight it. A second pop-up menu will appear.

3. Move the **mouse arrow** to the right and **click** on **Microsoft Excel**. The Welcome to Excel 97 screen will appear briefly before the main Excel window opens.

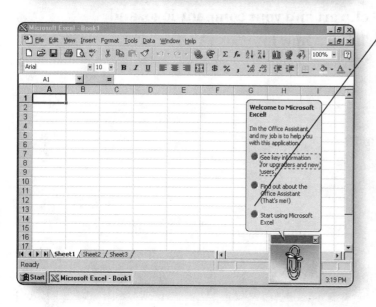

NOTE

If this is your first time using Excel, the Office Assistant appears with a balloon saying, "Welcome to Excel." Click on the blue button next to "Start using Microsoft Excel." If you're asked for a user name, type your name and initial in the dialog box and click on OK. For more information about working with Office Assistant, see the Getting Help section in Chapter 2, "What's on the Excel Screen."

ENTERING TEXT AND NUMBERS

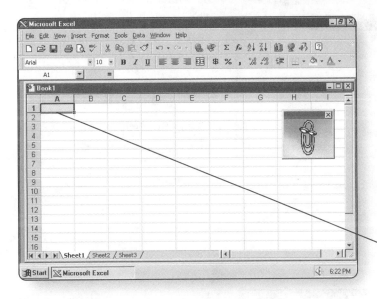

A spreadsheet is a rectangular grid of rows and columns. The columns are labeled with letters and the rows with numbers. The intersection of a row and a column is a *cell.* Each cell has an address, which is the column letter followed by the row number. For example, cell C10 is at the intersection of column C and row 10.

When you first open Excel, you'll notice that cell A1 has a border around it. This is the *active cell*.

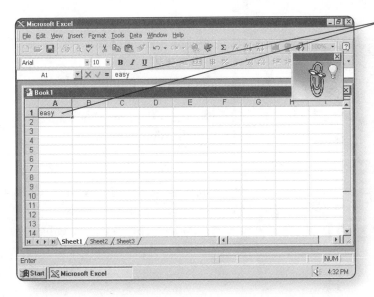

1. Type the word **easy** to enter text in the active cell. A flashing insertion point will appear at the end of whatever you type. You'll notice that what you type will appear not only in the active cell but also in the Formula bar.

NOTE

Text entries are called *labels*. Labels may contain any combination of letters, numbers, or symbols. Excel can only use numeric entries or values in a calculation. It cannot use labels.

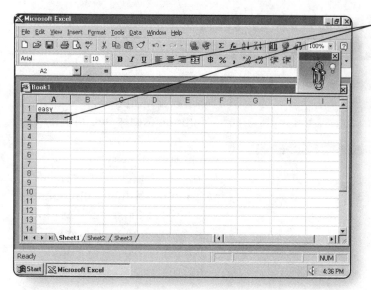

2. **Press** the **Enter key**. The cell below the current active cell will become the new active cell. The Formula bar will be empty again, because the new active cell is empty.

TIP

Another way to make a different cell active is to use the arrow keys on your keyboard.

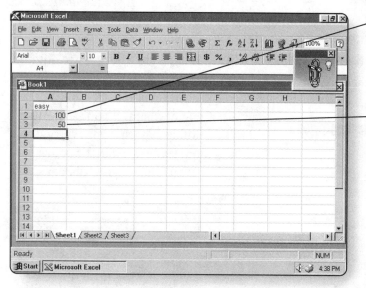

3. **Type** the number **100** in A2.

4. **Press** the **Enter key**. Cell A3 will be highlighted.

5. **Type** the number **50** in A3.

6. **Press** the **Enter key**. Cell A4 will be highlighted.

Notice that Excel right aligns the number in the cell. Excel left aligns *text* but right aligns *numbers*. This makes viewing different types of data easier.

ENTERING A FORMULA

In this section, you will create a simple formula in a single cell, which will add two numbers together. First, make sure the active cell is empty and located where you want the result of the formula to appear.

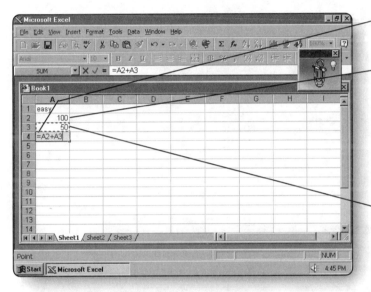

1. **Type** = (the equal sign) in the empty active cell.

2. **Click** on the **cell** that contains the **first number** you want to use in the calculation. The number will be added to the formula.

3. **Type** + (the plus sign).

4. **Click** on the **cell** that contains the **second number** you'd like to use in your formula. In the Formula bar, you will see the calculation that has been created.

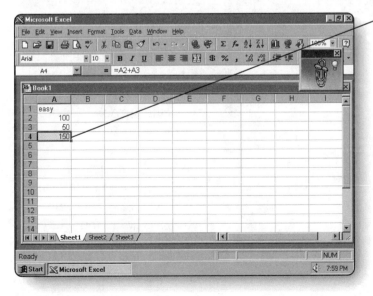

5. **Press** the **Enter key.** The formula will perform the calculation and the result will appear in the active cell.

If you move the pointer back up to the cell where the answer appears, you can see that the cell contains the result, but if you look at the Formula bar you can see that it still displays the formula you created.

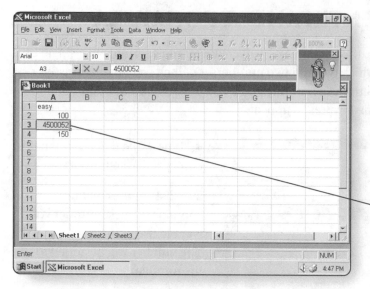

Playing What If?

The formula remains stored in the cell so you can change either of the numbers used in the calculation at any time.

1. **Click** on **cell A3.** The cell will be highlighted.

2. **Type** the number **4500052** over the number 50.

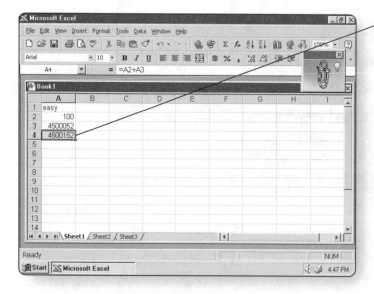

3. **Press** the **Enter key**. Excel will automatically recalculate the total.

Excel is able to perform the calculation because it not only displays the result in the cell, but it also stores the formula. The formula isn't 100 + 50, which is how you calculate on a calculator, but A2 + A3, which still appears in the Formula bar.

This is one of the main reasons why Excel is so powerful. Once you've set up a relationship between cells in a formula, you can change any of the numbers in those cells but the relationship in the formula remains.

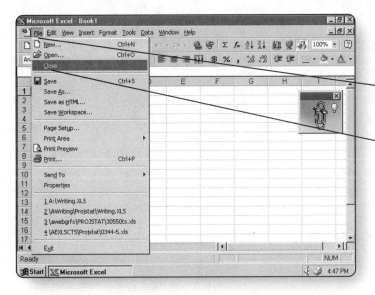

CLOSING A WORKSHEET

1. **Click** on **File**. The File menu will appear.

2. **Click** on **Close**. Office Assistant will ask if you want to save the changes to Book1.

3. **Click** on **No**. Your changes will not be saved.

TIP

For more information on closing worksheets and exiting Excel turn to Chapter 3, "Saving, Printing, and Exiting Excel."

2 What's on the Excel Screen?

A multitude of buttons and icons appear in the Excel window. Some of the icons make it easy to guess what the button does, however some are less obvious. This chapter helps you get comfortable working in the Excel screen. You'll learn how to:

- ✦ Use the toolbars and menu bar

- ✦ Work with options and dialog boxes

- ✦ Get help when you need it

- ✦ Change Clippit, if he's not your style

USING TOOLBARS

When you first look at the screen there appears to be an overwhelming choice of buttons to click on. How do you ever remember what all those symbols mean? Well, fortunately you don't really need to.

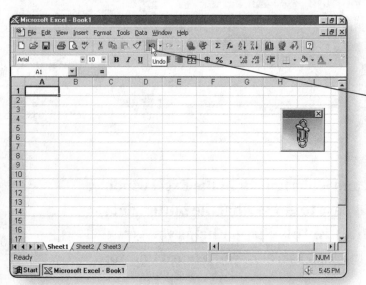

1. **Move** the **mouse arrow** over any button in the toolbar. The button name will be displayed.

Also if you look closely you can see that the buttons are grouped into related activities. For example, the Alignment buttons (left, center, right, and merge at center) are together.

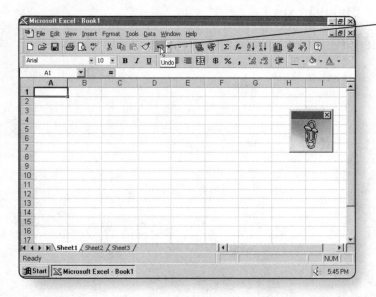

2. **Click** on a **specific toolbar button** to use it.

There are two toolbars displayed on this Excel screen. The one on top is the Standard toolbar, and the one below is the Formatting toolbar. There are other toolbars available but to view those you need to be able to use menus.

USING MENUS

1. **Click** on **Insert.** The Insert menu will appear.

To make a selection, simply click on an item in the list. As with the toolbars, related items are grouped together in the menus.

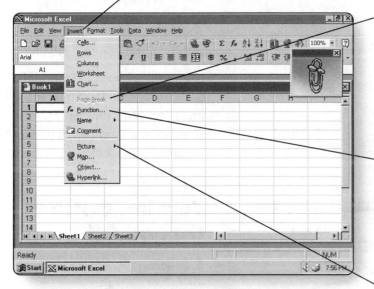

The menu item, Page Break, is dimmed because it is not available at this time. You probably need cells selected or at least some entries in the spreadsheet before you can use items which are dimmed.

Other menu items, such as Function, have icons indicating that there is a toolbar button for a selection. The icon on the menu is the exact same as the one on the toolbar.

When you see a right pointing arrowhead in a menu, it means another menu is available.

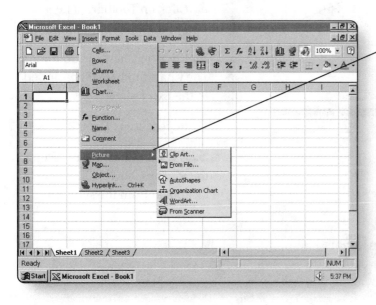

2. **Move** the **mouse arrow** over the arrowhead next to Picture. A second menu, which is called a *nested* or *submenu*, will appear.

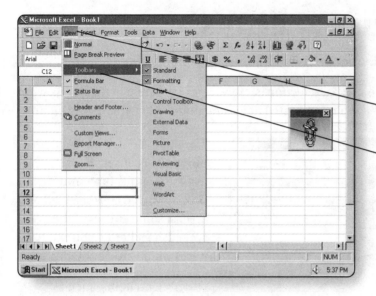

Selecting Options in Menus

1. **Click** on **View**. The View menu will appear.

2. **Click** on **Toolbars**. The Toolbars submenu will appear.

Notice the ✔'s next to Standard and Formatting. The Standard and Formatting toolbars are selected so they are open on the Excel screen.

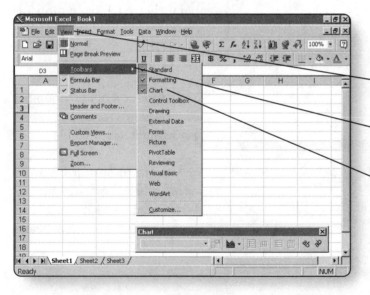

Turning Options On and Off

1. **Click** on **View**. The View menu will appear.

2. **Click** on **Toolbars**. The Toolbars submenu will appear.

3. **Click** on **Chart** to add a ✔. The Chart toolbar will be added to the Excel screen.

4. **Repeat steps 1** and **2**.

5. **Click** on **Chart** to remove the ✔. The Chart toolbar will disappear from the screen.

TIP

If you open a menu but don't want to make a selection, simply click anywhere on the screen outside of the menu box and the menu will close.

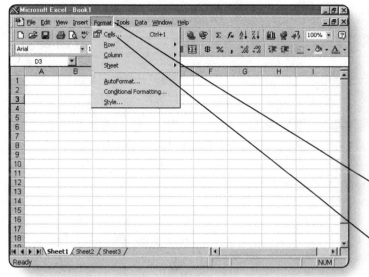

Working with Dialog Boxes

Many selections in the Excel menus are followed by three periods. The ellipsis indicate that, if you select an item, a dialog box will open.

1. **Click** on **Format**. The Format menu will appear.

2. **Click** on **Cells**. The Format Cells dialog box will appear.

Notice how related options have been grouped together on tabbed panels to make things easier to find. You can select from the groups, Number, Alignment, Font, Border, Patterns, and Protection.

3. **Click** on the **Alignment tab**. The Alignment options will appear.

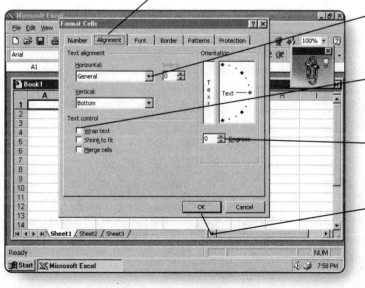

+ Select from drop-down lists by clicking on a down arrow (▾) like this one.

+ Turn features on or off by clicking on a box to insert or remove a ✔.

+ Adjust numbers in dialog boxes by clicking on up and down arrows like these (⬍).

4a. **Click** on **OK**. Selections made in the dialog box will be implemented.

OR

4b. **Click** on **Cancel**. The Format Cells dialog box will close and no changes will be made.

MOVING AROUND THE SCREEN WITH SCROLL BARS

There are several ways to move around an Excel worksheet.

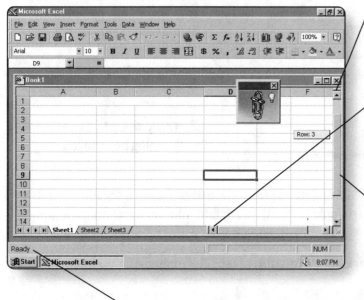

1. **Click repeatedly** on the **arrow** at either end of the vertical scroll bar to move the worksheet up or down in the window.

2. **Click repeatedly** on the **arrow** at either end of the horizontal scroll bar to move the worksheet left or right.

3. **Click** on the **vertical scroll box** and **hold** the **mouse button** while you **drag** the box up or down. Notice that when you move the scroll box, an indicator box will appear telling you which row you're scrolling over.

Below the horizontal scroll bar is the status bar. It tells you about operations in process in Excel. Most of the time it reads "Ready." When this setting is showing, you can work with the worksheet.

At the right end of the status bar is an indicator area which shows if the NUM lock for the numbers keypad, the CAP lock, or the Scroll lock are activated. If they are, an abbreviation appears in one of these boxes, such as CAPS or NUM. If they aren't active, the blocks are empty. In this screen, the NUM lock is activated.

GETTING HELP FROM OFFICE ASSISTANT

When you opened Excel 97 for the first time, what you probably noticed first was that cute animated paper clip trying to get your attention. That's Office Assistant, Excel's new Help feature.

1. **Click** on **Office Assistant**. The Office Assistant window will open.

2. **Type** in a **word** or two, reflecting what you might need help with, where it says, "Type your question here, and then click Search."

3. **Click** on **Search**. Another window will appear.

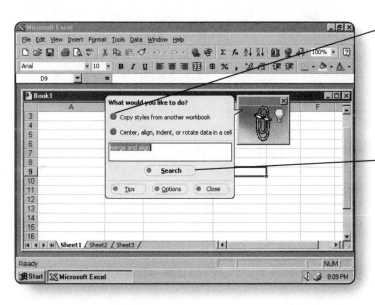

4. **Click** on the **topic button** representing the subject you need help with. You could also type in a different question at this point if none of the topics is useful.

5. **Click** on **Search**. Office Assistant will open the part of the Help database that addresses the topic you selected.

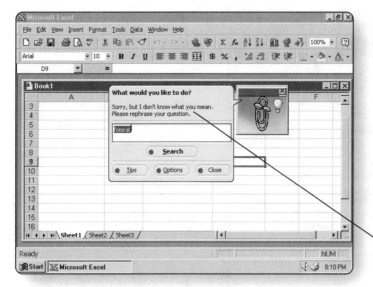

Frequently Office Assistant will open simply because you've performed particular keystrokes. In this situation, Office Assistant will immediately offer you context-sensitive help; options it thinks are related to the task you're performing.

If Office Assistant doesn't understand what you mean, it says it's sorry. Just try again. You probably just made a typing error.

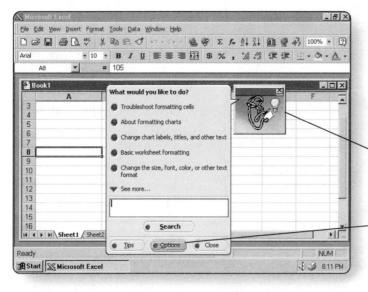

Having Fun with Office Assistant

Is the bendy paper clip, Clippit, getting a little dull or just not you're style?

1. **Click** on **Office Assistant**. The Office Assistant window will open.

2. **Click** on the **Options button**. The Office Assistant dialog box will open.

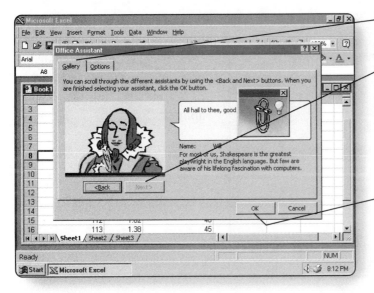

3. **Click** on the **Gallery tab**. The Gallery options will appear.

4. **Click** on **Next** to view the alternatives to the paper clip icon: The Dot, The Genius, Hoverbot, Mother Nature, Power Pup, Scribble (the cat), and Shakespeare.

5. **Click** on **OK**, when you find the one you want to use.

You're Office Assistant is always ready and willing to help!

TIP

Click on the Close button ([X]) on the top of Office Assistant to close Office Assistant. Press the F1 key on your keyboard to open Office Assistant, if it's not already available.

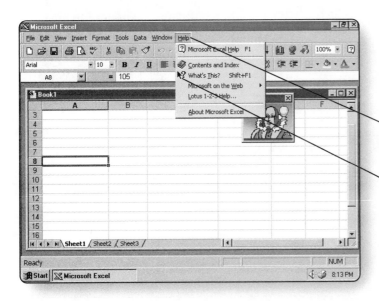

Using the Help Menu

1. **Click** on **Help.** The Help menu will appear.

2. **Click** on **What's This?** The mouse arrow will change to a black pointer with a question mark.

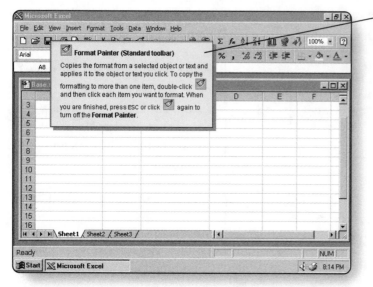

3. **Drag** the **pointer** over any button on the Excel screen and **click**. Excel Help will provide not only the name of the button but more detailed information about its function.

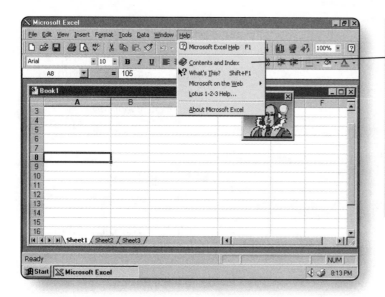

NOTE

The Contents and Index menu item provides a list of the contents of all the Help files for Excel. There is also an index to assist you in finding help. Instructions for finding help using Contents and Index are provided onscreen.

3 Saving, Printing, and Exiting Excel

Everyone who uses a computer has probably lost data at one time or another. If you haven't been saving to a disk regularly, you should remember that it only takes a few seconds to lose hours of work. You'll also probably want to make printouts of your work to share with others. You could use the hard copy as a report or possibly on a transparency as part of a presentation. In this chapter, you'll learn how to:

✦ **Save a worksheet**

✦ **Print your document**

✦ **Exit Excel**

SAVE, SAVE, AND SAVE AGAIN!

Computer users know they must save their work but many are guilty of forgetting, until something important is lost. Not only is it important to save your work so that you don't have to repeat it, but saving also gives you the opportunity to file your work electronically, so that you know where to find it.

1. **Click** on the **Save button**. If this is the first time you've saved the document, the Save As dialog box will open.

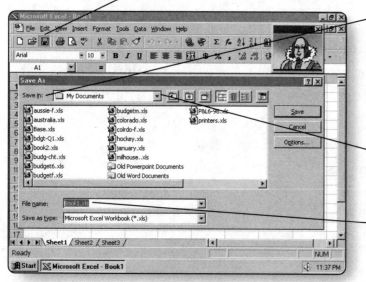

Save in: offers you a folder where you can save your worksheet. If you haven't made any changes to your software, the default folder that appears is the My Documents folder.

If you want to select a different disk or folder, click on the down arrow (▼).

2. **Type** a **name** for your file in the File name: text box. Excel will offer you "Book1" as a name. It's not a good idea to accept this because by the time you get to "Book9" it's going to be difficult to remember what exactly you saved in Book3 or 4.

3. **Click** on **Save**. Your document will be stored on a disk. Excel automatically adds an .xls extension to the filename. This indicates the file format used to save Excel files.

4. **Click** on the **Save button** regularly, to continue to save your document as you work on it. The Save As dialog box will not open again.

TIP

If you want to save a copy of your file with a different name, click on File and Save As to open the Save As dialog box again.

PRINTING A DOCUMENT

Whether you need to share a budget report with your colleagues or your retirement savings projection with your spouse, you need to print your file on paper.

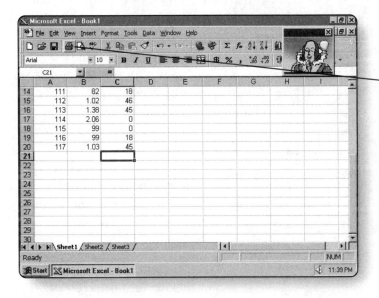

Printing with the Print Button

1. **Click** on the **Print button**. One copy of the worksheet that is currently open will be immediately sent to the printer.

Printing with the Print Dialog Box

If you'd like more control over what you're printing, if you'd like two copies of a workbook, or you only want to print the first four columns of your worksheet, you need to make selections in the Print dialog box.

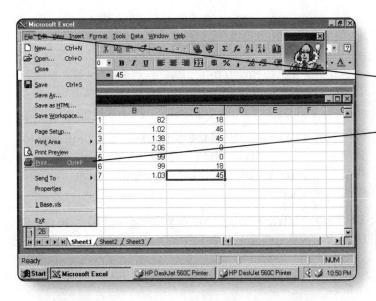

1. **Click** on **File**. The File menu will appear.

2. **Click** on **Print**. The Print dialog box will open.

3. **Choose** from the following **options**:

✦ If you are connected to more than one printer, you can choose the Name: of the printer to use for this print job by clicking on the down arrow (▼) and making a selection.

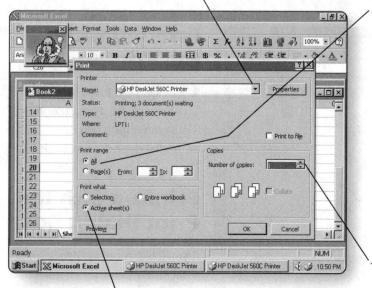

✦ Choose which pages of your document to print in the Print range box. You can print *All*, which is the pre-selected option, or if you only want to print a specific page, click on Pages. When you click on Pages, you can specify a range of pages to print. To do so, click on the up and down arrows (▲▼) to detail which page to print first and which page to stop printing at.

✦ Choose the Number of copies: to be printed by clicking the up and down arrows (▲▼) in the Copies box.

Another option in the Copies box is Collate. If you're printing more than one copy, you need to decide whether you want to collate. If you ✔ Collate, pages 1, 2, and 3, will be printed first, followed by another set of pages 1, 2, and 3. If Collate is not checked, three copies of page 1 will be printed, followed by three copies of page 2, and so on.

✦ In the Print what section of the dialog box, you can select to print a Selection of cells that you have highlighted, the Active worksheet—the one currently on the screen, or the Entire workbook.

4. **Click** on **OK**, when you've made your selections. The pages will be sent to the printer.

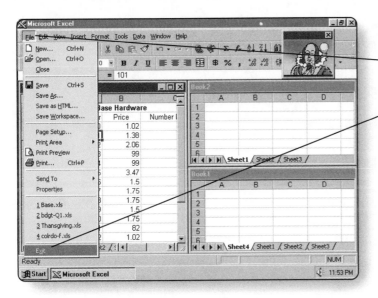

EXITING EXCEL

1. Click on **File**. The File menu will appear.

2. Click on **Exit**. If there are any workbooks opened that haven't been saved, Office Assistant will ask you whether or not you want to save changes to that particular file.

✦ **Click** on **Yes**, to save the workbook specified and exit. If you haven't previously saved the workbook, the Save As dialog box will open.

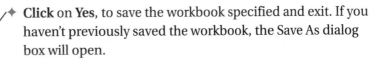

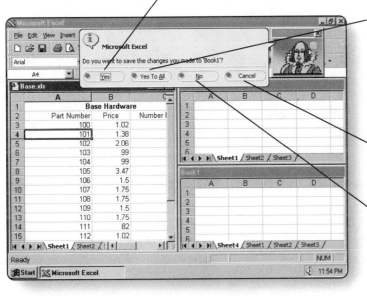

✦ **Click** on **Yes to All**, if you have more than one workbook open and want to save them all. If you haven't named any of the workbooks yet, the Save As dialog box will open.

✦ **Click** on **Cancel** to return to the Excel program without closing any workbooks.

✦ **Click** on **No**, to exit Excel without saving any changes.

4 Managing Workbooks and Worksheets

A workbook is an electronic file that contains one or more worksheets. The worksheets are like pages of a book which are available to you when your book (workbook) is open. Just as you can have different folders or books piled on the top of your desk at one time, you can have more than one workbook open at a time in Excel. You can easily switch between workbooks and worksheets as well. In this chapter, you'll learn how to:

✦ Create a new workbook

✦ Open and close workbooks

✦ View multiple workbooks

✦ Add, name, and delete worksheets

OPENING A NEW WORKBOOK

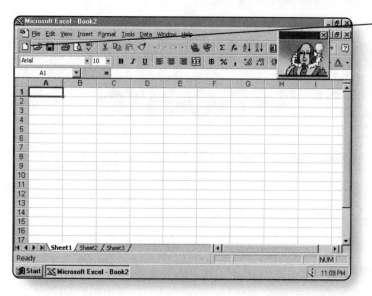

1. Click on the **New button**. A new worksheet will open with the title "Book2," but your title could be different because it reflects how many workbooks you've created during this session.

MOVING BETWEEN WORKBOOKS

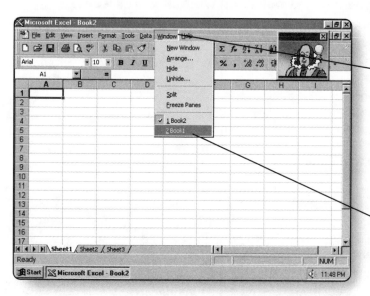

1. Click on **Window**. At the bottom of the Window menu is a list of the files you have open. The file with the ✔ next to it is the file that you are currently working on in the main Excel window.

2. Click on the **filename** of the file you want to work with. The file you specify will be displayed onscreen.

VIEWING MULTIPLE WORKBOOKS

In Excel, you can have more than one workbook open and view more than one workbook onscreen at a time. You can also view workbooks tiled on the screen with the screen divided into multiple windows, one for each workbook.

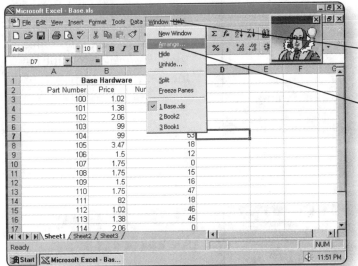

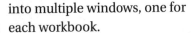
1. Click on **Window**. The Window menu will appear.

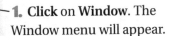
2. Click on **Arrange**. The Arrange Windows dialog box will appear. It will ask you if you want to tile the workbooks, show all the workbooks vertically across the screen, horizontally, or cascade one title bar under the next.

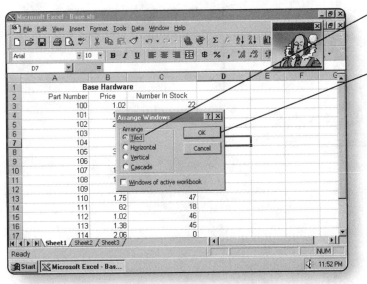

3. Click on **Tiled**. The item will be selected.

4. Click on **OK**. The workbooks will be tiled onscreen.

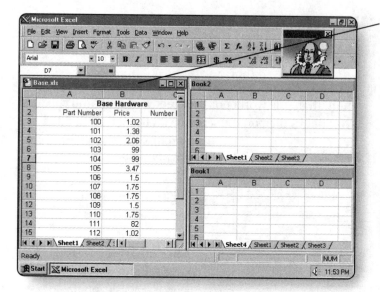

You can work in any of the workbooks by clicking in it, to make it active. Use the scroll bar to move quickly through the worksheet data.

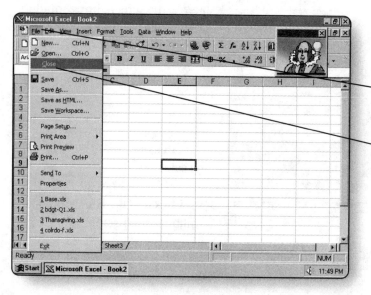

CLOSING A WORKBOOK

1. Click on **File**. The File menu will appear.

2. Click on **Close**. Office Assistant will appear and ask if you want to save changes.

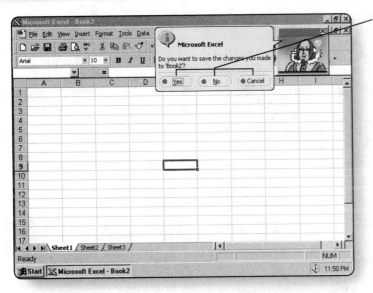

3. Click on **Yes** to save changes, click on **No** to close the workbook without saving, or click on **Cancel** to go back to the workbook.

OPENING AN EXISTING WORKBOOK

There are two ways to open an existing workbook (a workbook that has previously been saved on a disk). If you've been working on a the workbook recently, it will probably still be listed at the bottom of the File menu. If it's not listed, you'll need to search for its location on a disk.

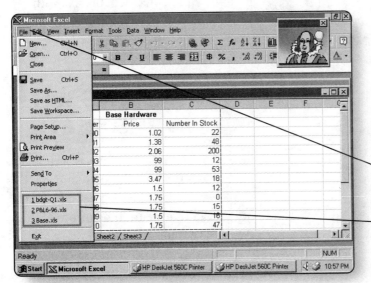

Opening with the File Menu

1. Click on **File**. The File menu will appear.

2. Click on the **worksheet** you want to work on. The worksheet will appear onscreen.

Opening with the Open Button

1. **Click** on the **Open button**. The Open dialog box will appear.

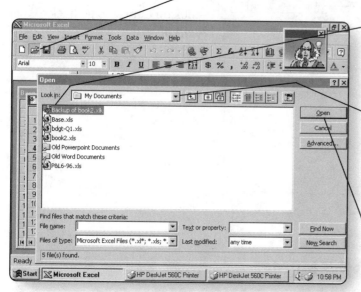

2a. **Click** on the **file** you want to open. The file will be highlighted.

OR

2b. **Click** on the **down arrow** (▾) in the Look in: box to select the disk or folder where your file is saved. When you find the file you want to open, highlight it by clicking on it once.

3. **Click** on **Open**. The selected file will appear onscreen.

NOTE

You can also open a file by clicking on the File menu and then on Open. Browse with the Open dialog box to locate the file you want.

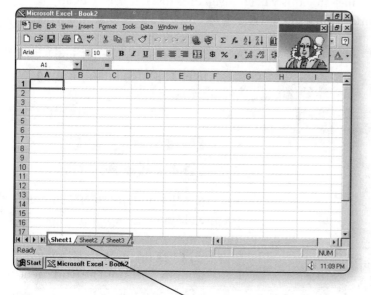

WORKING WITH WORKSHEETS

By default, each new workbook has three worksheets, and each worksheet has a Sheet tab, which you can see at the bottom of the workbook window.

1. **Click** on a **worksheet tab** to move to a different worksheet.

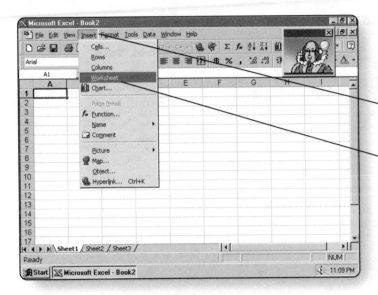

Adding Worksheets to a Workbook

1. **Click** on **Insert**. The Insert menu will appear.

2. **Click** on **Worksheet**. A new worksheet will be added to your workbook.

NOTE

All of the worksheets are saved each time you save the workbook.

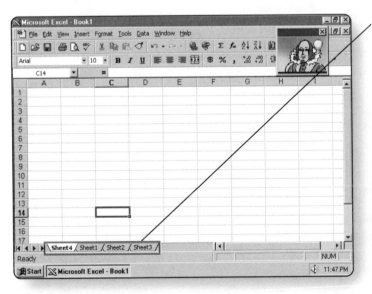

Notice that the new worksheet is added to the left of the worksheet that is currently active or open on the screen.

TIP

You can rearrange the order of the tabs on the screen by clicking on one of the tabs and dragging it to a new location.

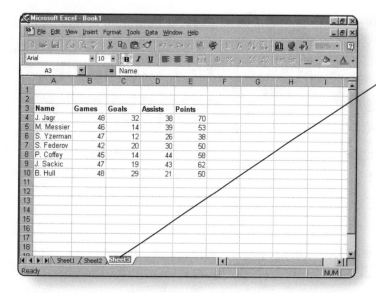

Naming a Worksheet

1. **Click twice** on the **tab** for the sheet you want to name. The current name will be highlighted and ready for editing.

2. **Type** a **new name**.

3. **Click anywhere** outside of the tab. The name change will appear on the tab you selected.

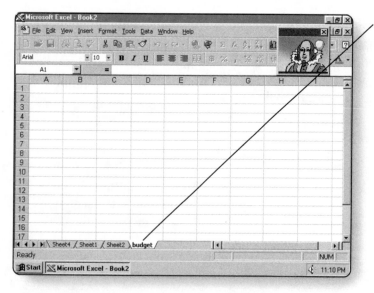

Notice the new name for the worksheet on the tab you selected.

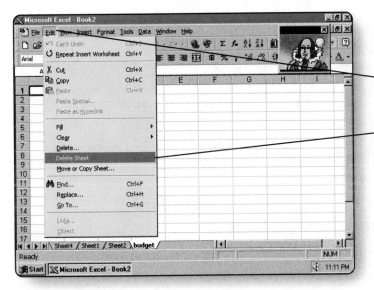

Deleting a Worksheet

1. Click on **Edit**. The Edit menu will appear.

2. Click on **Delete Sheet**. A dialog box from Office Assistant will open and tell you that the sheet will be permanently deleted.

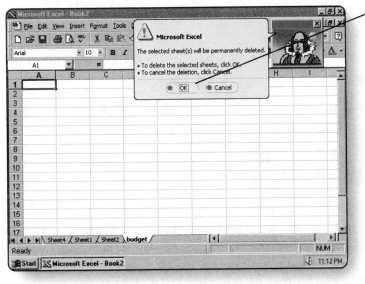

3. Click on **OK**. The worksheet will be deleted.

PART I REVIEW QUESTIONS

1. In Excel, what does C10 mean? *See "Entering Text and Numbers" in Chapter 1.*

2. In Excel, what are labels? *See "Entering Text and Numbers" in Chapter 1.*

3. Why is entering a formula in Excel better than using a calculator? *See "Playing What If?" in Chapter 1.*

4. How can you display toolbars other than the Standard and Formatting toolbars in Excel? *See "Selecting Options in Menus" in Chapter 2.*

5. What word must appear in the status bar before you can work with a worksheet? *See "Moving around the Screen with Scroll Bars" in Chapter 2.*

6. How can you save an extra copy of a file? *See "Save, Save, and Save Again!" in Chapter 3.*

7. What happens when you click on the Print button? *See "Printing with the Print Button" in Chapter 3.*

8. What is the difference between a workbook and a worksheet in Excel? *See the introduction in Chapter 4.*

9. How can you tell Excel which workbook you want to work in when you have several open at one time? *See "Viewing Multiple Workbooks" in Chapter 4.*

10. When you insert a new worksheet into a workbook, where does Excel insert the new worksheet? *See "Adding Worksheets to a Workbook" in Chapter 4.*

PART II

Constructing Larger Worksheets

5 Editing Worksheets

When you create a worksheet, there's a lot of data entry involved. Excel has features to cut down on at least some of that repetitive work. Unfortunately, you'll still make mistakes, so you need to know how to edit cell entries, run spell-check, and you'll probably want to make some changes to the way you construct your worksheet. There are some great features in Excel that allow you to reorganize your worksheet without having to re-enter any data. In this chapter, you'll learn how to:

- ✦ Select and edit cells
- ✦ Delete data, rows, and columns
- ✦ Copy and move data
- ✦ Fill and transpose ranges
- ✦ Adjust column width and row height
- ✦ Spell-check a worksheet

SELECTING CELLS

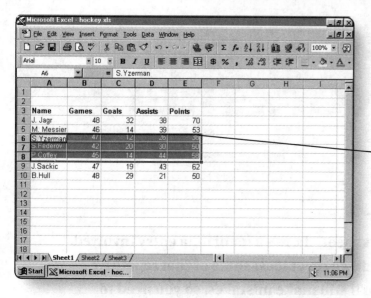

Before you can work with many of the features in Excel you need to know how to select cells. You can select a rectangular group of cells, called a *range*, in any of the following ways:

✦ **Click** and **drag** over the selection.

✦ **Click** in **one cell**, and then **hold down** the **Shift key** and **click** in the **opposite corner** of the selection.

✦ **Click** on the **Select All button**, the gray rectangle where the column and row headings meet, to select the entire worksheet.

✦ **Click** in a **column** or **row heading** to select the whole column or row.

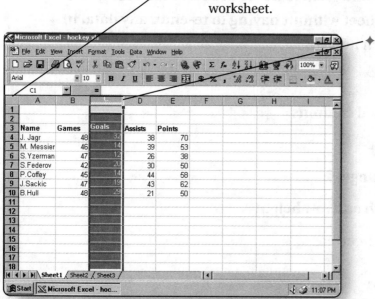

EDITING DATA

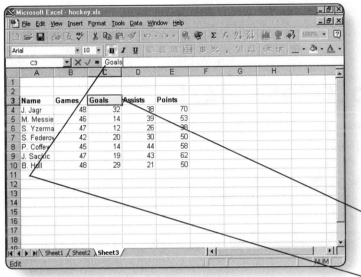

When you enter new information in the Formula bar you can edit it before you press the Enter key. You can delete characters using the Backspace key. You can also move the insertion point with the arrow keys and either insert text by typing or delete text by pressing the Delete or Backspace keys.

1. **Click** on a **cell**. The cell will be highlighted.

2. **Click** in the **Formula bar** to place the insertion point anywhere in the entry. You will now be able to insert or delete text.

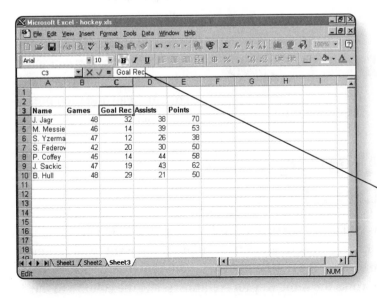

3. **Press** the **Backspace key**. The character to the immediate left of the insertion point will be deleted.

4. **Press** the **Delete key**. The character to the right of the insertion point will be deleted.

5. **Click** in the **Formula bar** to place the insertion point anywhere in the entry.

6. **Type** new **text**.

> **NOTE**
> Characters are inserted to
> the left of the insertion point.

DELETING DATA

There are a number of different ways you can delete data in a
worksheet:

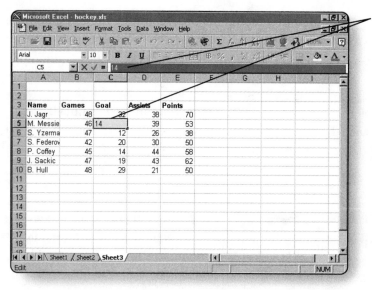

♦ If you want to totally replace
the original entry in a cell,
simply click on the cell and
then type. The text in the
Formula bar will be selected
and anything you type will
replace the selection.

♦ The fastest way to delete the
contents of a cell or range of
cells is to select the cell or
cells and press the Delete key.

♦ If you want to delete an entire
row or column, you can select
it by clicking in the row or
column head and then press
the Delete key.

ADDING ROWS AND COLUMNS

As you construct your worksheet, you'll occasionally find that
you need to add rows and columns. If you want to add a new
row, select the row below where you want to add the new row.
It works the same way for columns: select the column to the
right of where you want to add a new column.

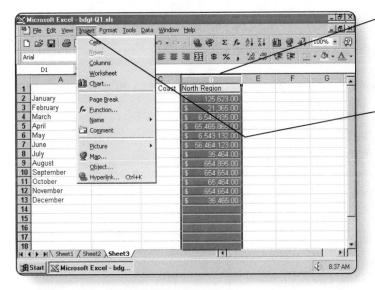

1. Click in a **row** or **column head** to select it. The row or column you choose will be highlighted.

2. Click on **Insert**. The Insert menu will appear.

3. Click on **Rows** or **Columns**. The new row or column will be inserted before the row or column you initially selected.

NOTE
Depending on whether you select a row or column, the menu item for a row or column will be either available or dimmed.

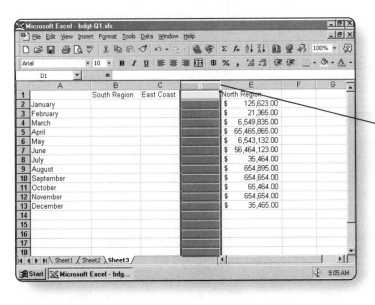

Notice that Column D becomes column E and a new column D is displayed.

OOPS!–USING UNDO AND REDO

Sometimes you'll want to undo an action you've just completed in Excel.

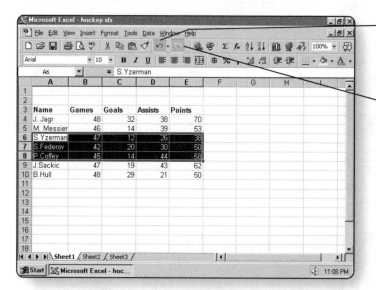

1. **Click** on the **Undo button**. The last action you performed will be undone.

2. **Click** on the **Redo button** to reverse the action.

TIP

If you've made a mistake by undoing, immediately click on the Redo button to get back what was undone.

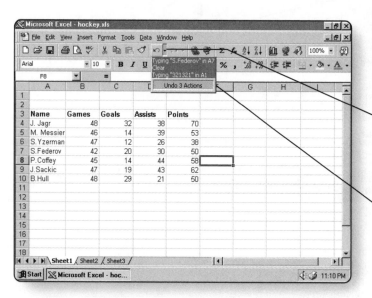

After working in a worksheet for a while there will be many levels of Undo that you can work back through.

3. **Click** on the **down arrow** (▼) next to the Undo button. You will see your recent actions listed.

4. **Click** on the **action** (or series of actions) you want to undo. Your selection will be highlighted and the action(s) will be deleted.

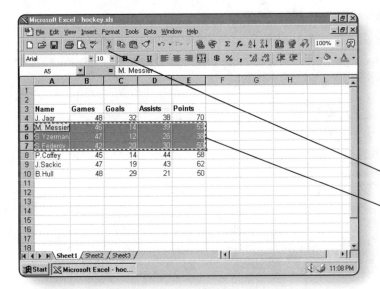

MOVING DATA

One of the advantages of using Excel is the ease with which you can move and copy data.

1. **Select** a **range of cells**. The cells will be highlighted.

2. **Click** on the **Cut button**.

Marching ants seem to be running around your selection. Notice that your data doesn't disappear like text does when cut in a word processor. You can still see the data you're working with.

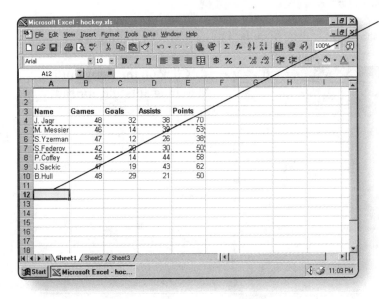

3. **Click** in the **cell** which will be the upper left corner of the new location of the range.

NOTE

There must be enough empty cells in the new location to accommodate the cut data or else existing data will be overwritten.

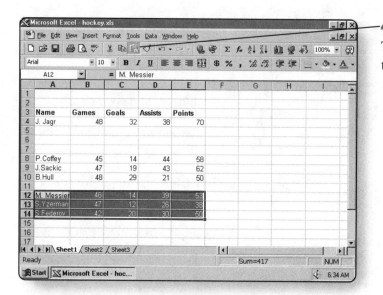

4. **Click** on the **Paste button**. The pasted data will appear in the new location.

COPYING DATA

1. **Select** a **range of cells**. The cells will be highlighted.

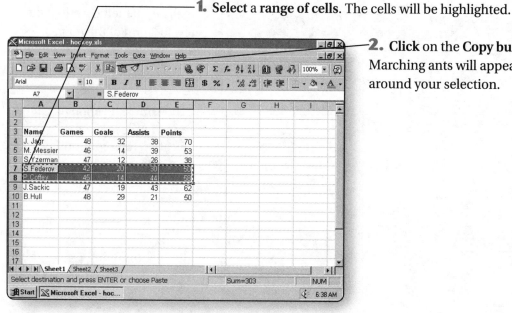

2. **Click** on the **Copy button**. Marching ants will appear around your selection.

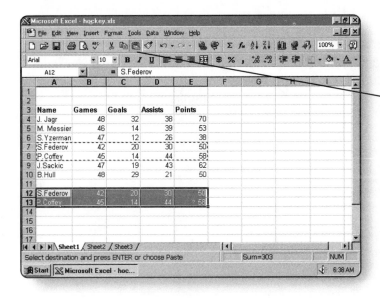

3. **Click** in the **cell** at the top left of the range where you want to place the copy.

4. **Click** on the **Paste button**. The selected range will appear in both the original location and the new location.

Using Drop and Drag

A quick way to move data, if you're good with a mouse, is by using the Drag and Drop feature.

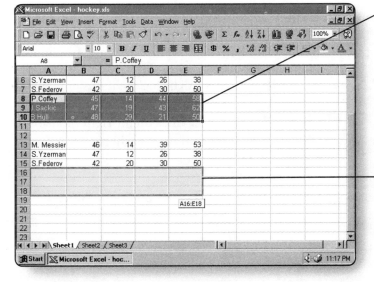

1. **Select** the **cells** you want to move. The cells will be highlighted.

2. **Click** with the **mouse arrow** anywhere on the border of the rectangle, except on the fill handle at the lower right corner.

3. **Press** and **hold** the **mouse button** as you **drag** the cells to a new location. The cell location you're dragging over will appear in a box below the mouse arrow.

NOTE

For information about using the Fill Handle, see the section on "Filling a Range" later in this chapter.

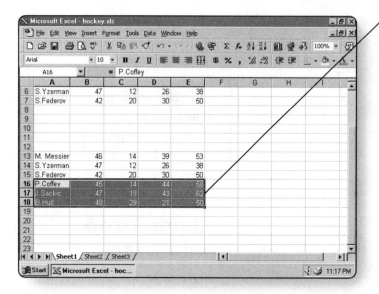

4. **Release** the **mouse button.** The cells will be dropped in the new location. This is much quicker than using buttons or menus!

Using the Shortcut Menu

You've probably wondered why the mouse has two buttons when you only seem to use the left one. Well, there are times when you can use the right one.

1. **Select** some **cells**. The cells will be highlighted.

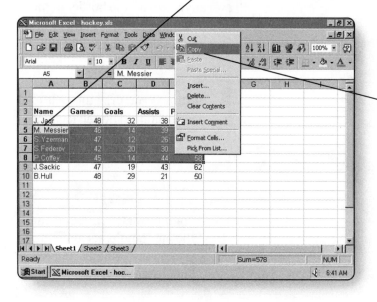

2. **Click** on the **right mouse button.** The shortcut menu will appear.

3. **Click** on **Cut** or **Copy**.

4. **Click** in the **cell** where you want to paste the selection. The cell will be highlighted.

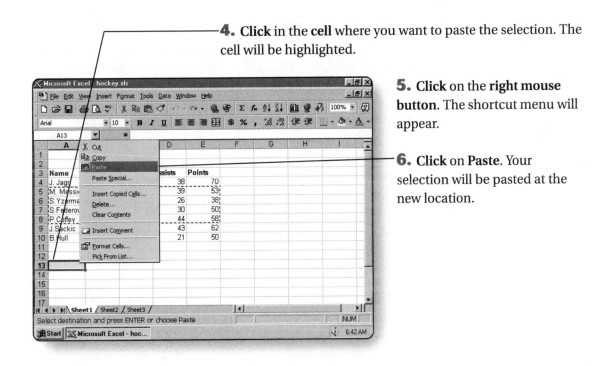

5. **Click** on the **right mouse button**. The shortcut menu will appear.

6. **Click** on **Paste**. Your selection will be pasted at the new location.

FILLING A RANGE

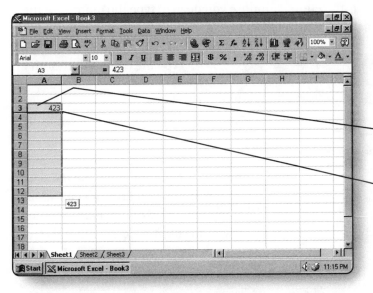

The Fill feature is for those people who hate data entry. Excel can't do all the data entry for you but it can do some of those repetitive tasks.

1. **Select** a **cell**. The cell will be highlighted.

2. **Click** on the **Fill Handle** (the extra little square on the bottom right corner of the highlighted cell). Notice that the mouse arrow changes to a plus sign.

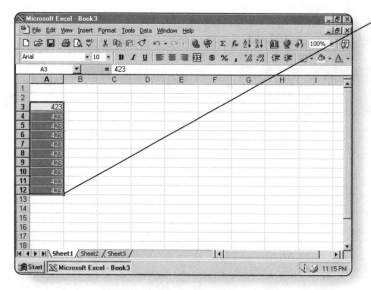

3. Press and **hold** the **right mouse button** and **drag** the **Fill Handle** to the right or down a number of cells.

4. **Release** the **right mouse button**. The original contents of the highlighted cell, whether it was a number or a formula, will be copied to all the cells you selected.

NOTE

There is more coverage of copying formulas in Chapter 6, "Using Formulas and Functions."

Not only can you fill a range with a number or formula but you can do it with a series. This is really how this feature saves you time and effort. Suppose you need to type the months of the year to construct a budget.

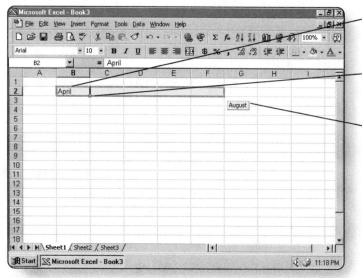

1. **Type** the **name** of a month in a cell.

2. **Click** on the **Fill Handle** of that cell.

3. Press and **hold** the **mouse button** and **drag** the **Fill Handle** to the right. You don't even need to count the cells because as you drag, Excel shows you exactly which month you're on!

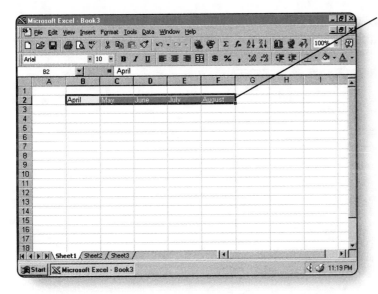

4. Release the **mouse button**. The months of the year following the one you typed in will be automatically inserted.

TRANSPOSING CELLS

Imagine you've entered five columns of data. Your fingers are aching from all that data entry, but now you realize that you don't really want the names in a row across the top of the worksheet. The worksheet would be much more effective and easier to work with, if the names were in a column. In this situation, you use the Transpose feature. The Transpose feature switches rows of cells to columns or columns to rows.

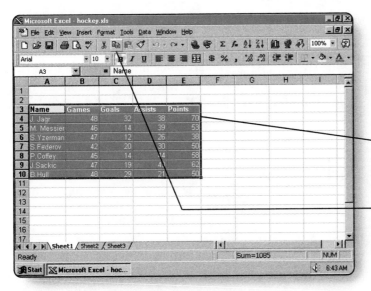

1. Select the **cells** you want to transpose. The cells will be highlighted.

2. Click on the **Copy button**. The cells you selected will be copied to the Clipboard.

TIP

Be sure to select all the data you need even if it doesn't show immediately on the screen.

3. Click in the **cell** that will be the top left corner of your new range. The cell will be highlighted.

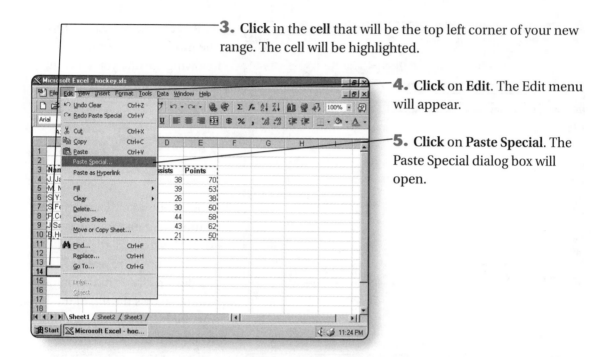

4. Click on **Edit**. The Edit menu will appear.

5. Click on **Paste Special**. The Paste Special dialog box will open.

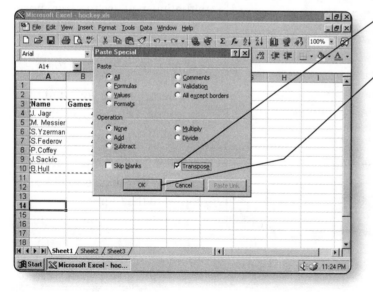

6. Click on **Transpose**. A ✔ will be put in the box.

7. Click on **OK**. The dialog box will close.

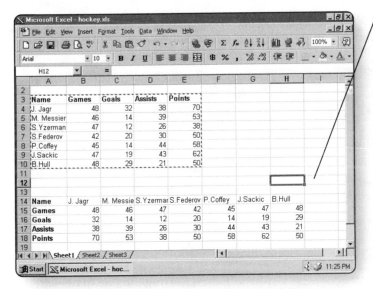

The entire table is displayed in the new location with rows converted to columns, and columns to rows.

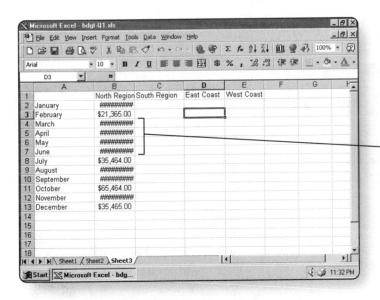

ADJUSTING COLUMN WIDTH AND ROW HEIGHT

Column width is something you quickly learn you need to adjust. When numbers are too wide to show in a cell in a worksheet, a series of # signs is displayed.

1. Move the **mouse arrow** to the boundary between the column headings on the right side of the column you want to adjust.

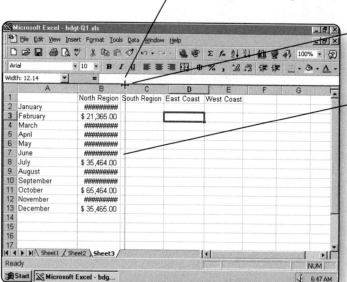

2. Click on the **line**, when the mouse arrow changes to a double-headed arrow.

3a. Press and **hold** the **mouse button** and **drag** the **line** to the right to widen the size of the cells in the column.

OR

3b. Drag the **line** to the left, if you want to shrink the size of the column.

4. Release the **mouse button**. The changes will take effect.

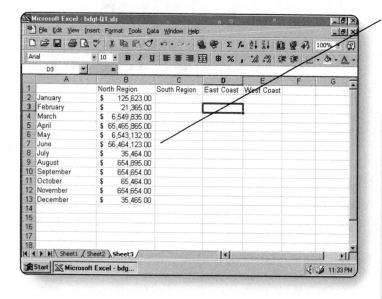

Once the column is wide enough, the entire number will be displayed.

TIP

If you want to increase row height, move the mouse arrow to the line between the rows and when the mouse arrow changes to a double-headed arrow, click and drag the line to increase or decrease the size of the row. Try increasing row height to draw attention to a row or add a large font in a heading.

CHECKING YOUR SPELLING

Once you've entered all your data you will probably want to print your worksheet to share it with others. Before you take that step, it's a good idea to check your spelling. Even if you always won the spelling bee at school, you probably make the occasional typing error, and the spell-check feature may catch it. However, be aware that it doesn't catch all mistakes. If you've made a typing or spelling error, such as using "led" instead of "lead," since both words are in the dictionary, Spelling will not flag this as an error. Therefore, it is still very important to proofread your work.

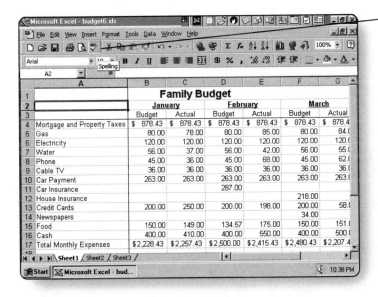

1. **Click** on the **Spelling button**. The Spelling dialog box will open.

NOTE

If Excel doesn't find any errors, a dialog box will open that tells you the spell-check is complete.

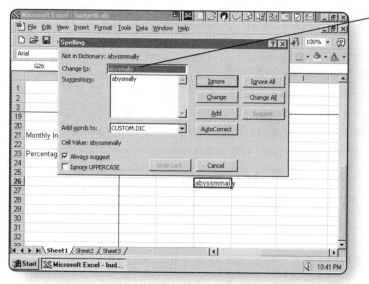

At the top of the dialog box next to Not in Dictionary:, Excel identifies the first item it can't match. There are suggestions listed with the first suggestion appearing in the Change to: text box.

2. Choose from the following **options**:

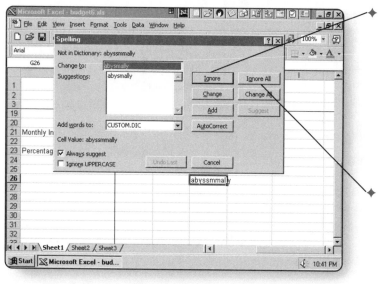

✦ **Ignore.** If the word highlighted is spelled correctly but is flagged because it does not appear in the dictionary (which often happens with proper names), click on this option to move to the next misspelling without making any changes.

✦ **Ignore All.** If the highlighted word is likely to continue to occur and is spelled correctly, click on this option to ignore all future occurrences.

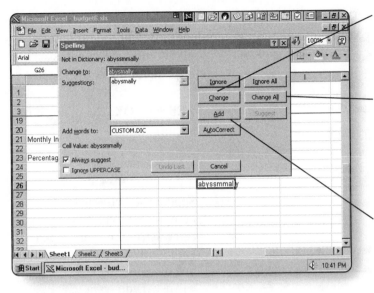

◆ **Change.** This option will change the misspelled word to the option displayed in the Change to: text box.

◆ **Change All.** This option will change this occurrence and all subsequent occurrences of the highlighted word to the option displayed in the Change to: text box.

◆ **Add.** If the word is spelled correctly and you do not want Excel to continue to identify this word as a misspelling every time you run spell-check, click on Add to add the word to the dictionary.

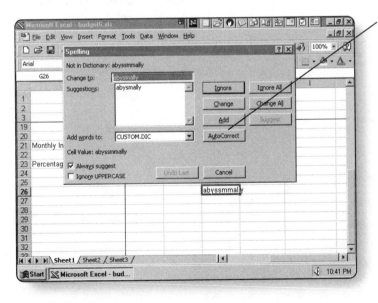

◆ **AutoCorrect.** If a word you often misspell or mistype is identified, type the correct spelling in the Change to: text box. If you aren't sure of the spelling, click on Suggest, and then click on the correct spelling in the Suggestions list. You can now add the misspelled word to the list of automatic corrections by clicking on AutoCorrect. Now as you enter the word in your worksheet, it will be automatically corrected if you type or spell it incorrectly.

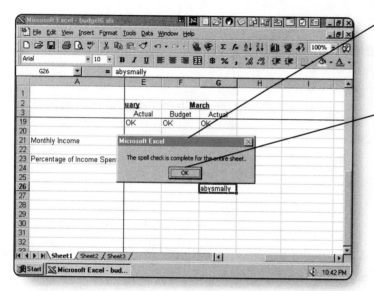

After Spelling is finished, a dialog box will appear telling you that the spell-check is complete for the entire sheet.

3. **Click** on **OK.** The dialog box will close.

NOTE

Spelling searches from the active cell down. If the active cell wasn't at the very top of your worksheet when you began spell-check, Spelling will ask if you want to continue spell-checking at the beginning of the sheet when it reaches the bottom of the worksheet.

6 Using Formulas and Functions

Merely entering large quantities of data into a worksheet isn't
going to help you a great deal. You need to perform calculations on
that data to summarize it in a useful way. For example, you might
find it helpful to know how much you really spent this year on your
car or phone bill. You can then apply the information to plan,
budget, find trends, or make predictions. In this chapter, you'll
learn how to:

✦ Use the Formula palette and functions to perform calculations

✦ Copy formulas with relative and absolute cell references

✦ Use Goal Seek to find information you need

✦ Use AutoCalculate and cell comments

✦ Correct errors in formulas

ENTERING A SIMPLE CALCULATION

To add, subtract, multiply, or divide numbers, you can use formulas. Formulas use cell references combined with the addition (+), subtraction (-), multiplication (*), and division (/) operators to perform calculations.

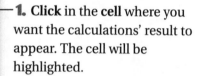

1. Click in the **cell** where you want the calculations' result to appear. The cell will be highlighted.

2. Click on the **Edit Formula button** (the equal sign) in the Formula bar. An equal sign will appear in the selected cell and in the Formula bar. Every formula has to start with an equal sign or Excel thinks you are just entering data.

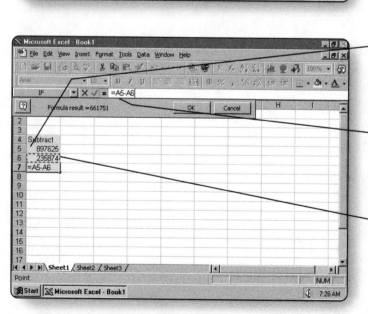

3. Click on the **cell** with the first number you want to use. Excel will enter the cell address in the selected cell and Formula bar.

4. Type an **operator**. The operator you type will appear in the selected cell and in the Formula bar.

5. Click on the **cell** with the next value you want to use in your calculation. Excel will enter the cell address in the selected cell and Formula bar.

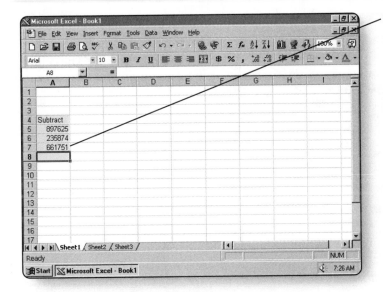

6. **Press** the **Enter key**. The result will be displayed in the selected cell.

USING BUILT-IN FUNCTIONS

Many calculations have been pre-defined in Excel. These built-in calculations are called *functions*. The easiest way to include a function in your worksheet is by using the Formula palette.

Using the Formula Palette with the SUM Function

The Formula palette keeps track of the functions you enter, and displays a description of the formula and how it's constructed.

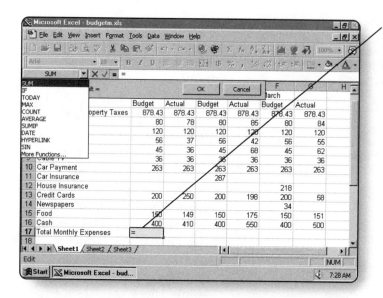

1. **Click** in the **cell** where you want the result of your calculation to appear. The cell will be highlighted.

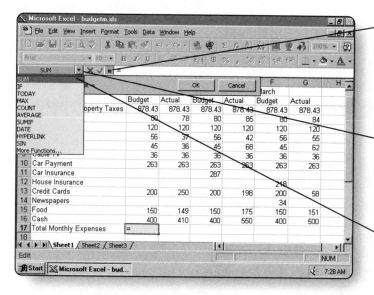

2. **Click** on the **Edit Formula button**. An equal sign will appear in the selected cell and Formula bar, and the Formula palette will open.

3. **Click** on the **down arrow** (▼) to the right of the Function box to select a function. A drop-down menu will appear.

4. **Click** on **SUM**. The Formula palette will expand to provide help with the calculation.

TIP

If you want a total at the bottom of a column of data, click in the cell at the bottom of that column.

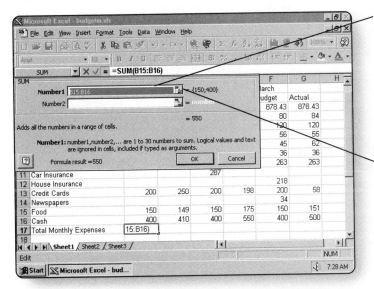

Notice that in the Number1 text box Excel has tried to guess which numbers you're trying to add. Unfortunately, as the column in this example does not have a number in every cell, the guess is wrong.

5. **Click** on the **Collapse Dialog button** at the end of the Number1 text box to edit the formula. The Formula palette will shrink to allow you to see your worksheet and select the range of cells for the calculation.

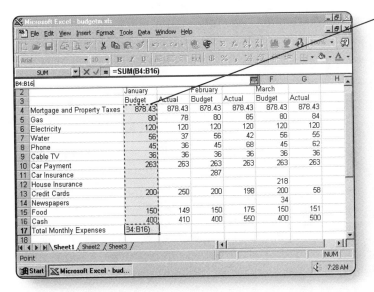

6. **Select** the **cells** to be included in your calculation. Marching ants will highlight your selection and a range will appear in the Formula bar.

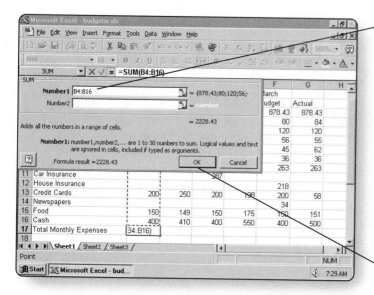

7. **Press** the **Enter key**. The Formula palette will expand with your selection entered in the Number1 text box.

8. **Click** on **OK**, if the calculation in the Formula bar is correct. Your formula will be entered.

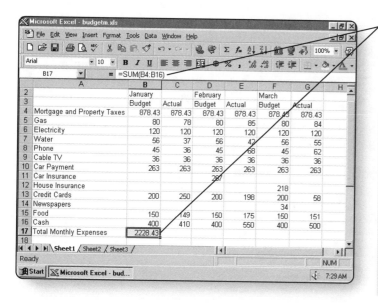

You can view the formula in the Formula bar and the total of the calculation in the selected cell.

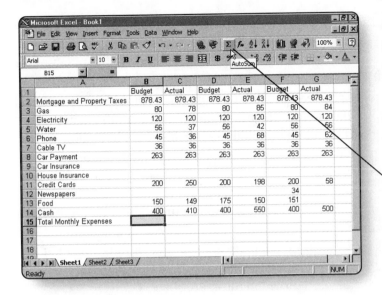

Adding a Column of Numbers

1. **Click** in the **cell** where you want a result. The cell will be highlighted.

2. **Click** on the **AutoSum button**. Excel will suggest the range to be added.

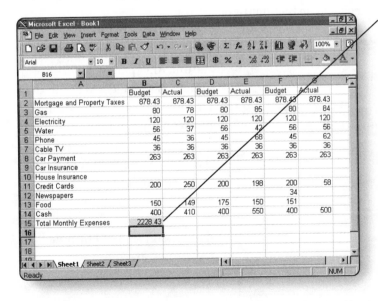

3. **Press** the **Enter key**, if the range Excel suggests is correct. The result of the AutoSum is entered in the selected cell. If the suggested range is not correct, drag through the range you want before pressing the Enter key.

Using the Formula Palette with the IF Function

All functions work in basically the same way. You enter the equal sign, select the function, and then tell the function which data to use. The next example demonstrates using a logical function rather than a mathematical one. Logical functions use the =, >, <, >=, <=, and <> operators within a formula to test if something is true or false.

If the function is true one result is returned; if false, another is returned. In the following example, a "Warning" is returned if it's true that you spent more than $200 to pay off your credit card account in a month. If it's false and you spent less than $200, "OK" is returned in the appropriate cell.

1. **Click** in the first **cell** where you want the warning to appear. The cell will be highlighted.

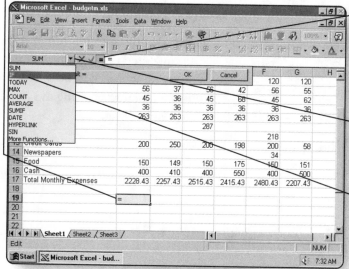

2. **Click** on the **Edit Formula button**. An equal sign will appear in the selected cell and Formula bar, and the Formula palette will open.

3. **Click** on the **down arrow** (▼) to the right of the Function box. A drop-down menu will appear.

4. **Click** on **IF**. The Formula palette will expand.

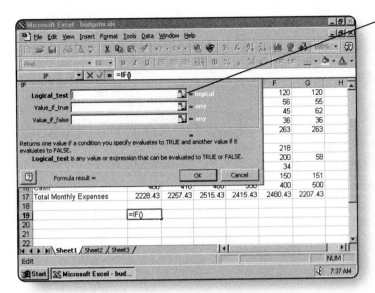

5. Click on the **Collapse Dialog button** at the end of the Logical_test text box. The Formula palette will shrink.

6. Select data **cells**. The cells will be highlighted with marching ants.

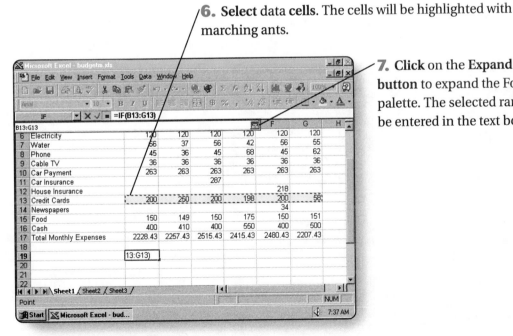

7. Click on the **Expand Dialog button** to expand the Formula palette. The selected range will be entered in the text box.

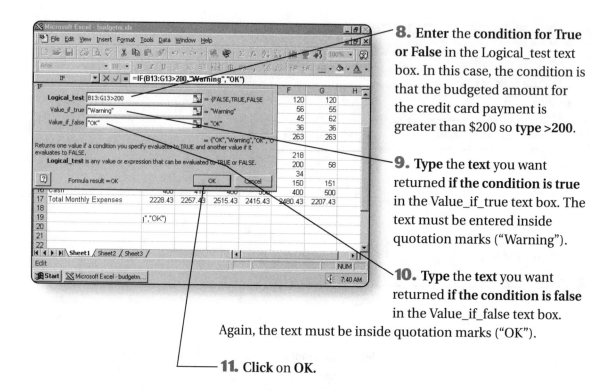

8. **Enter** the **condition for True or False** in the Logical_test text box. In this case, the condition is that the budgeted amount for the credit card payment is greater than $200 so **type >200**.

9. **Type** the **text** you want returned **if the condition is true** in the Value_if_true text box. The text must be entered inside quotation marks ("Warning").

10. **Type** the **text** you want returned **if the condition is false** in the Value_if_false text box. Again, the text must be inside quotation marks ("OK").

11. **Click** on **OK**.

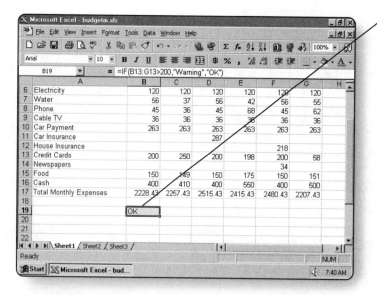

The function result will be entered into the worksheet.

12. Click on the **Fill Handle** and **drag** across a row or column to copy the formula. Results will appear in the cells.

A "Warning" will appear in the columns where the credit card payment is larger than the $200 budgeted.

COPYING FORMULAS WITH RELATIVE AND ABSOLUTE REFERENCES

Formulas are copied from one cell to another just like you copy any other data. However, in the section above when the cell with the formula was copied into other cells in the worksheet using the fill handle, the formula that was copied was *relative*. What this means is the formula in column B calculates using numbers from cells in column B. Similarly, the formula in column C, even though it was copied from column B, calculates using numbers entered in column C.

This figure shows the formula entered in cell B19.

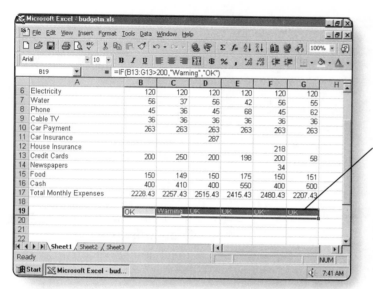

TIP

See Chapter 5, "Editing Work-sheets," for more information on using Copy, Paste, and Fill.

This figure shows that same formula as it appears when copied from cell C19.

Most of the time you will want Excel to copy formulas in this way. However, there may be times when you want an *absolute* cell reference. An absolute cell reference is one which does not change depending on location. If you have a formula with an absolute reference to cell B3, which you then copy from B17 to D17, the formula in D17 will still contain the reference to B3.

Suppose you want to calculate the percentage of your income that you are spending each month. You don't need to enter your income in each column, if it's always the same you can use an absolute cell reference.

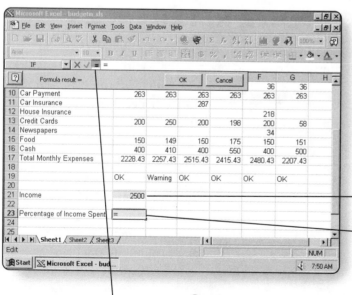

1. Type a **number** in a cell.

2. **Click** in the **cell** where you want the calculation to appear. The cell will be highlighted.

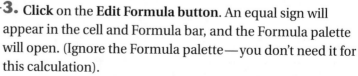

3. **Click** on the **Edit Formula button**. An equal sign will appear in the cell and Formula bar, and the Formula palette will open. (Ignore the Formula palette—you don't need it for this calculation).

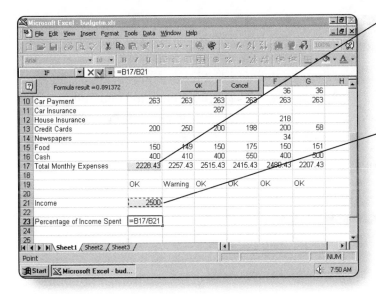

4. Click in the **cell** with the total for monthly expenses.

5. Press the **/ key** to indicate that you want to divide.

6. Click in the **cell** with the total for monthly income.

7. Click on the ✔ or press the **Enter key**. The formula will be entered.

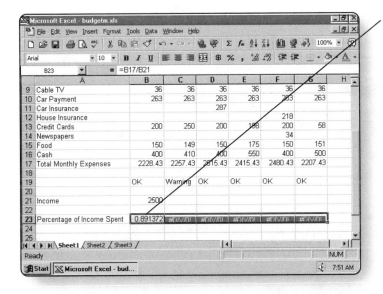

The percentage will appear in the calculation cell you selected.

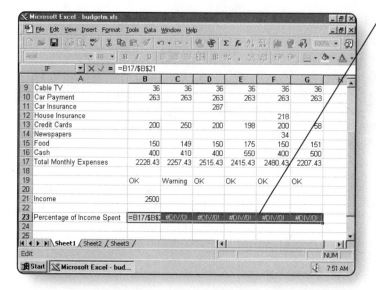

If you copy this formula across the worksheet, you won't get a percentage for each month because there is not any income entered in the remaining columns. You get an error message (#DIV/0!).

8. Click in the **cell** where you entered the formula. The formula will be displayed in the Formula bar.

9. Click in the **Formula bar** to place the insertion point in front of the letter of the cell reference which you want to make absolute.

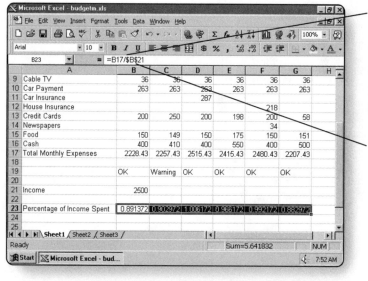

10. Type $.

11. Press the **right arrow key** to move the cursor in front of the row number of the cell reference that you are making absolute.

12. Type $ again.

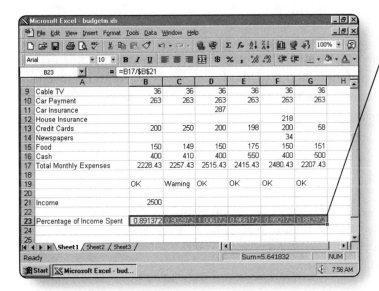

13. Press the **Enter key**.

14. Drag the **cell with the formula** across the worksheet. The percentage income will calculate for each month.

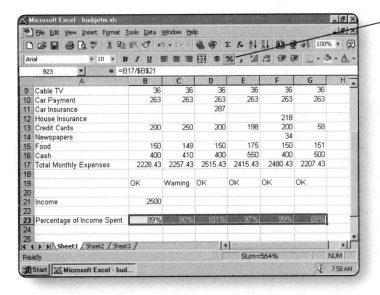

15. Click on the **Percent Style (%) button.** This will quickly format the numbers in the selected cells. The numbers don't look much like percentages until they are formatted.

TIP

To find out more information on how to format numbers see Chapter 13, "Formatting Numbers and Cells."

USING THE GOAL SEEK TOOL

The Goal Seek tool enables you to find a result by adjusting one of the cells in a worksheet. First, you need to specify a goal and then tell Excel what cell's value it can adjust to meet that goal.

Suppose you wanted to be sure that your expenses don't exceed your income. However, in the example worksheet February's budget is in excess of the monthly income of $2,500. Therefore, your goal is to reduce monthly expenses to $2,500. The amount you spend on food is one item in the budget that you can control, you can select this as the adjusting cell.

1. **Click** in the **cell** that you want to change to the new goal value. The cell will be highlighted.

2. **Click** on **Tools**. The Tools menu will appear.

3. **Click** on **Goal Seek**. The Goal Seek dialog box will open.

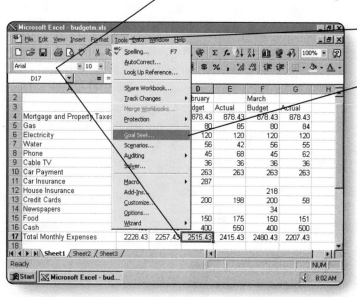

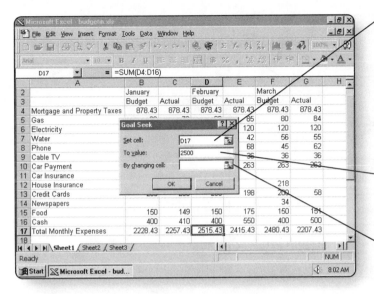

The address of the cell that will contain the goal value should already appear in the Set cell: text box. If not, type in the correct cell reference.

4. Click in the **To value: text box**.

5. Type the **new goal value** for the cell mentioned in the Set cell: text box.

6. Click on the **Collapse Dialog button** for By changing cell:. You will return to the worksheet.

7. Click in the **cell** that you want to adjust. In this case, the cell with the amount spent on food entered.

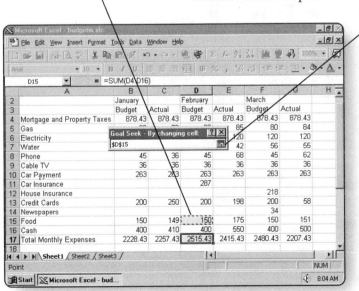

8. Click on the **Expand Dialog button**. The Goal Seek dialog box will expand.

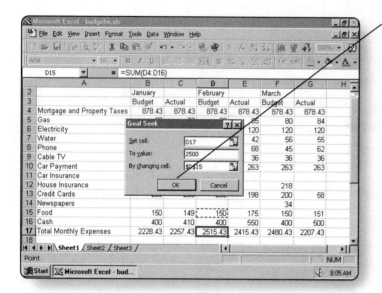

9. **Click** on **OK**. The worksheet will recalculate.

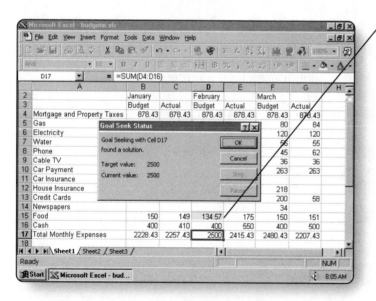

Excel will enter the specific goal in the selected cell and automatically adjust the value in the other specified cell. In this case, if you want expenses to be no greater than your income, then in February, you can only spend $134.57 on food.

USING AUTOCALCULATE

You might find that occasionally you want to know the sum or average of a group of numbers, but don't really need to record the information in a worksheet. You can perform a quick sum, average, count, max, or min calculation using AutoCalculate.

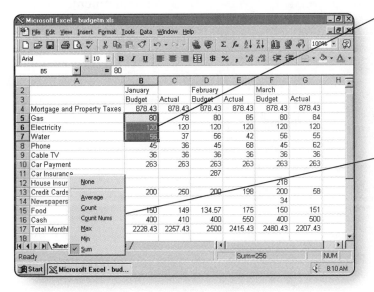

1. **Select** the **cells** containing the values you would like to calculate. The cells will be highlighted.

2. **Point** to the **status bar** with the mouse arrow.

3. **Click** on the **right mouse button**. A pop-up menu will appear.

4. **Click** on a **function** to put a ✔ by it. The result of the calculation will appear in the status bar.

ADDING COMMENTS

When you begin to build larger more complex calculations it is sometimes useful to be able to include an explanation of what you've done, but you may not want those explanations cluttering up your worksheet. One way to add information is to include a comment.

1. Click on the **cell** where you want to include the comment. The cell will be highlighted.

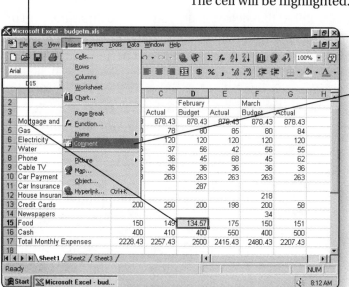

2. Click on **Insert**. The Insert menu will appear.

3. Click on **Comment**. A text box will open with a flashing insertion point.

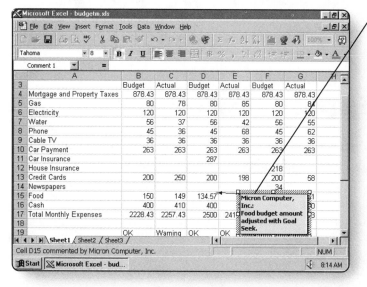

4. Type your **comment**.

5. Click **anywhere** outside of the comment box. The comment box will disappear but a tiny red triangle will appear in the top right corner of the cell.

NOTE

To view the comment, move the pointer over the triangle and the comment box will be displayed.

SOME COMMON MISTAKES TO AVOID

The Formula palette helps beginners avoid mistakes, but you'll probably still make a few. When you make a mistake there are a number of error messages that might appear. The following are the most common:

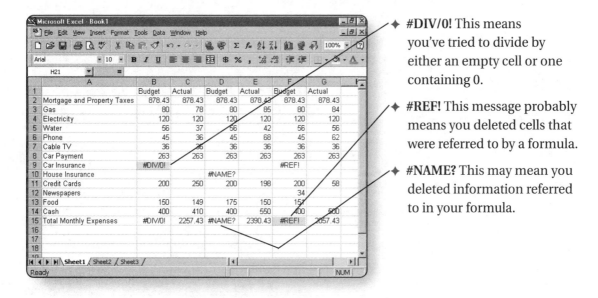

✦ **#DIV/0!** This means you've tried to divide by either an empty cell or one containing 0.

✦ **#REF!** This message probably means you deleted cells that were referred to by a formula.

✦ **#NAME?** This may mean you deleted information referred to in your formula.

When you check your formulas, some things to watch for are that:

✦ Formulas start with an equal sign.

✦ All the necessary parentheses are included.

✦ You referred to the correct cells.

✦ You've included all the arguments and no extra arguments.

7 Navigating Your Worksheets

As you create larger worksheets, it's possible to get lost in the flood of data and not know exactly where you are. Fortunately, Excel has features to help you work with larger worksheets. In this chapter, you'll learn how to:

✦ Name a range

✦ Move directly to a specific cell or range

✦ Find and replace entries in your worksheet

✦ Hide and display rows and columns

✦ Split your Excel window and freeze parts of a worksheet

NAMING A RANGE

Naming a range is useful because names are easier to read and remember than cell addresses. Named ranges can be used to quickly select text and move around a worksheet in combination with the Go To command. They can also be used in formulas.

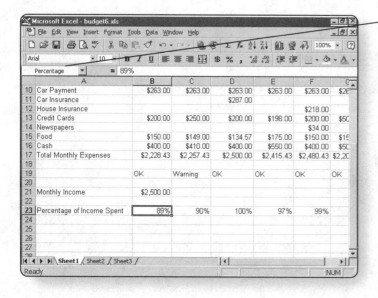

1. Click in a **cell** or **drag** the **mouse arrow** across a **range** of **cells**. The cell(s) will be highlighted.

2. Click in the **Name text box** to the left of the Formula bar. The text box will be highlighted.

3. Type a **name** for the highlighted cells.

4. Press the **Enter key**. The name will appear in the Name text box.

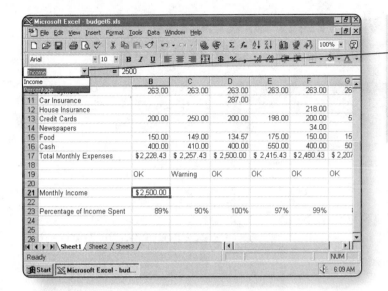

TIP

To quickly select a named cell or range, click on the down arrow (▼) at the end of the Name text box and select from the drop-down list.

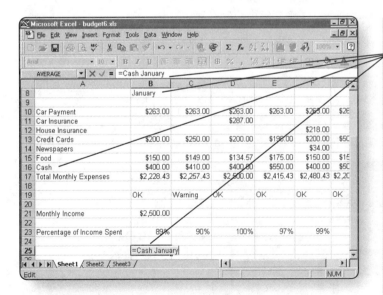

NOTE

You can also use column and row labels in a worksheet to refer to data in formulas. For example, if you have a column headed "January" and a row with the label "Cash," you can find the cash balance for January by entering the formula "=Cash January." The space between Cash and January is called the *intersection operator*. It tells the formula to return the value in the cell at the intersection of the row labeled "Cash" and the column labeled "January."

MOVING DIRECTLY TO A CELL OR RANGE

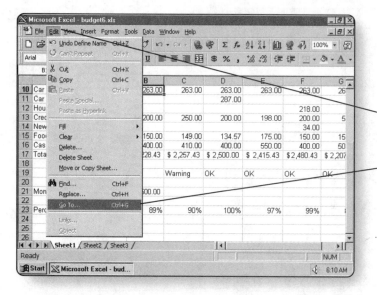

When you've got thousands of entries in your worksheet, moving with the arrow keys or scroll bar can be frustrating.

1. **Click** on **Edit**. The Edit menu will appear.

2. **Click** on **Go To**. The Go To dialog box will open.

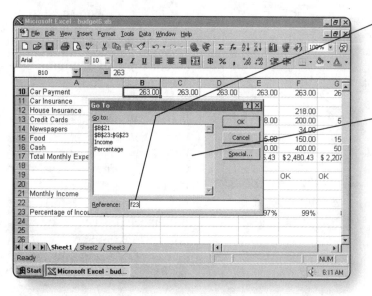

3a. **Type** a **cell address** in the Reference: text box.

OR

3b. **Click** on a **range name** from the Go to: list.

4. **Click** on **OK**. The Go To dialog box will close.

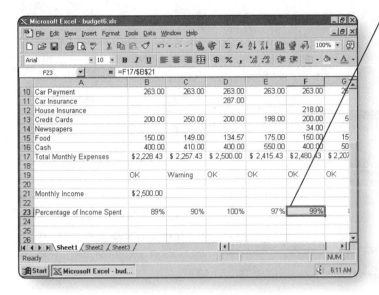

The cell or range you specified will become the active cell or selected range.

TIP

To move to the last cell that contains data in a worksheet, press the Ctrl and End keys at the same time. To move back to the first cell (A1), press the Ctrl and Home keys at the same time.

FINDING AND REPLACING CELL ENTRIES

If you need to update your worksheet (maybe interest rates have increased), you can use the Find or Replace commands to help you.

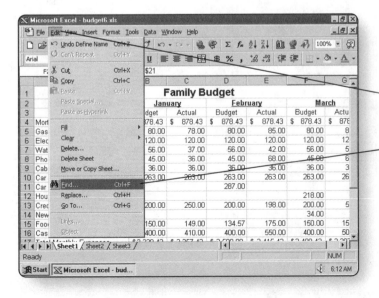

Finding Cell Entries

1. **Click** on **Edit**. The Edit menu will appear.

2. **Click** on **Find**. The Find dialog box will open.

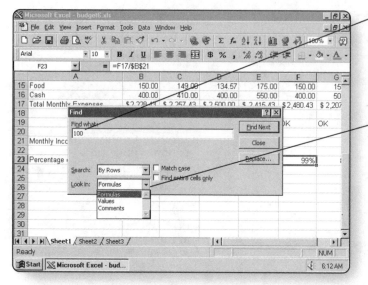

3. Type the **word** or **number** you want to find in the Find what: text box. Be sure to enter it exactly as it was originally entered into the worksheet.

4. Click on the **down arrow** (▼) next to the Look in: text box. The Look in: drop-down list will appear.

5. Click on **Formulas**, **Values**, or **Comments**, depending on what kind of data you want Find to search.

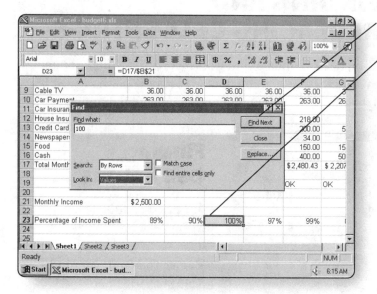

6. Click on **Find Next**.

Excel will find the first occurrence of the word or number. You can continue to click on Find Next until all occurrences have been identified.

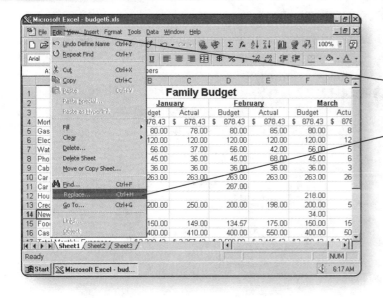

Replacing Cell Entries

1. **Click** on **Edit**. The Edit menu will appear.

2. **Click** on **Replace**. The Replace dialog box will open.

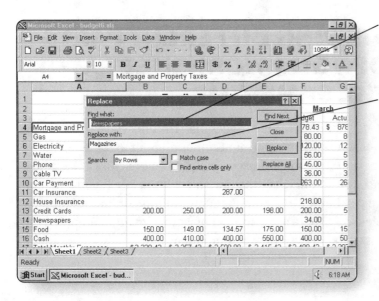

3. **Type** the **word** or **number** you want to replace in the Find what: text box.

4. **Type** the **revised entry** in the Replace with: text box.

NOTE

At this point, you can click on Replace All and immediately replace all occurrences of the original entry with the new one. However, it's not a good idea to do this if you're not an experienced user. You may replace something you didn't intend to replace.

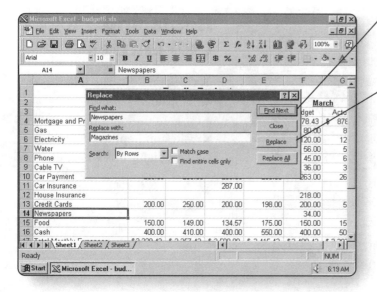

5. Click on **Find Next**. Excel will find the first occurrence of the word or number.

6a. Click on **Replace**, if the item found is one you wish to replace.

OR

6b. Click on **Find Next**.

7. Repeat steps **5** and **6** until you've checked all occurrences of the word or number in the worksheet.

VIEWING DIFFERENT PARTS OF YOUR WORKSHEET AT THE SAME TIME

Once your worksheet is bigger than the area you can see on your screen at one time, it becomes difficult to remember where exactly you are as you move down or across a worksheet and can no longer see the row and column labels you entered. Are you in the January or February column, or the cash or sales row? There are a number of ways of manipulating a worksheet to overcome this problem.

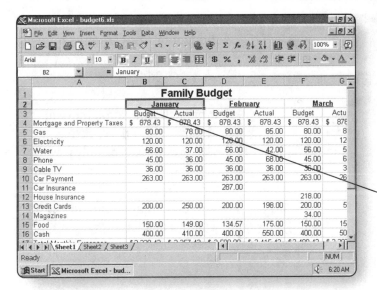

Hiding Rows and Columns

If there are columns or rows that you've set up that you really don't need to work in anymore, or that you don't want to print, you can hide them.

1. **Click** in the **cell**(s) where you want to hide rows or columns. The cell(s) will be highlighted.

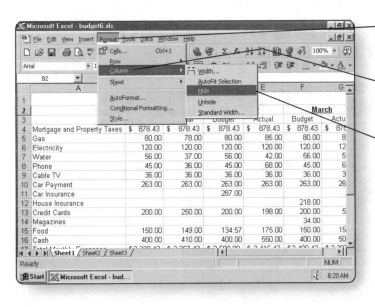

2. **Click** on **Format**. The Format menu will appear.

3. **Click** on **Column** or **Row**. A submenu will appear.

4. **Click** on **Hide**.

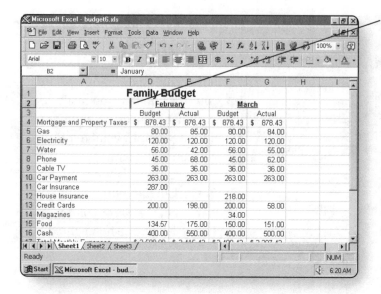

Initially, a dark vertical or horizontal line will appear between the columns or rows you have hidden.

Notice that once you move in the worksheet the dark line disappears and the only way to tell that rows or columns have been hidden, is by the missing letters or numbers in the row or column headers.

Displaying Hidden Rows or Columns

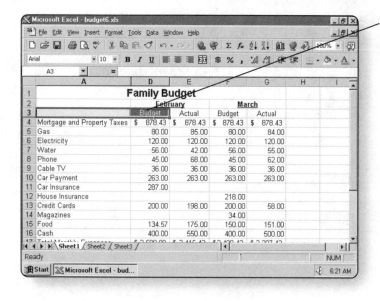

1. Select the **cells** on both sides of the missing rows or columns. The cells will be highlighted.

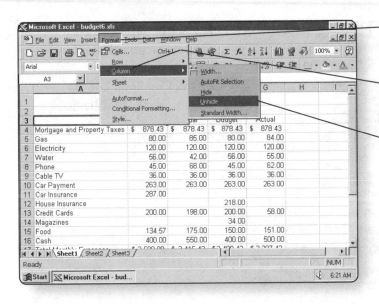

2. Click on **Format**. The Format menu will appear.

3. Click on **Column** or **Row**. A submenu will appear.

4. Click on **Unhide**.

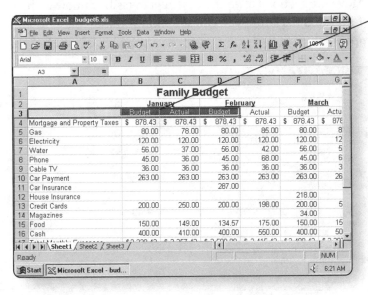

The missing columns or rows will reappear.

Splitting a Window

If you want to see particular sections of the same worksheet, but the worksheet is so big you can't view both sections onscreen at the same time, you can split a window.

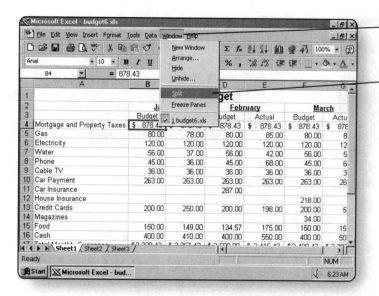

1. **Click** on **Window**. The Window menu will appear.

2. **Click** on **Split**. The spreadsheet will be divided into four sections.

3. **Move** the **sections** of your worksheet in each window with the four scroll bars until you can see what you want to compare.

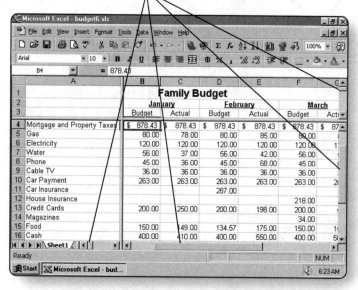

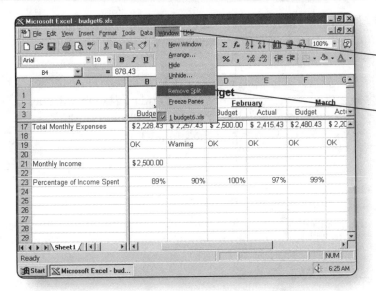

Removing a Split

1. Click on **Window**. The Window menu will appear.

2. Click on **Remove Split**. The split will be removed.

Keeping Row or Column Labels Visible

When you're entering data you need to know which row and column you're on. The letters and numbers Excel provides are not very informative. You need to be able to see the labels you set up for certain columns and rows, like months of the year or employee names. You can do this by freezing columns and rows that contain labels you need to see all of the time.

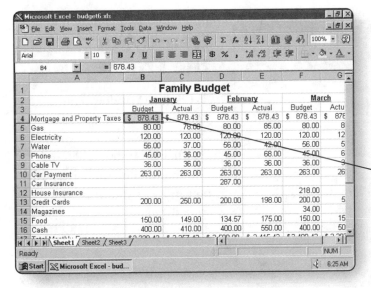

1. Click in the **cell** below the column labels and to the right of the row labels. The cell will be highlighted.

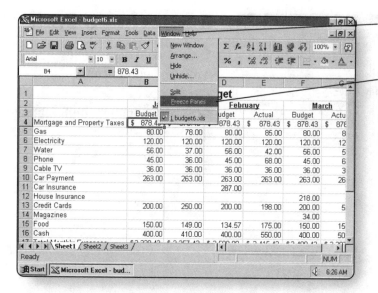

2. **Click** on **Window**. The Window menu will appear.

3. **Click** on **Freeze Panes**. The column and row labels will stay onscreen while you work with the spreadsheet.

Notice when you scroll left and right through your data, the column containing the row labels remains onscreen. When you scroll up and down through your data, the row containing the column labels remains frozen onscreen. However, if you scroll left and right, the column labels move and if you scroll up and down, the row labels move.

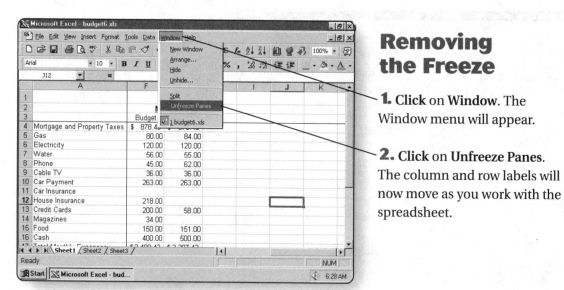

Removing the Freeze

1. **Click** on **Window**. The Window menu will appear.

2. **Click** on **Unfreeze Panes**. The column and row labels will now move as you work with the spreadsheet.

8 Using Macros

Whenever you find yourself repeating the same keystrokes again and again, you can probably benefit from a macro. A *macro* is simply a recording of keystrokes, and in the same way that you play recordings of music, you can play macros. In this chapter, you'll learn how to:

✦ Create and name a macro

✦ Run a macro

✦ Delete a macro

RECORDING AND NAMING YOUR MACRO

Before recording a macro, plan what you intend to include. If you make mistakes while recording, all the mistakes will be recorded along with the correct keystrokes.

1. Click on **Tools**. The Tools menu will appear.

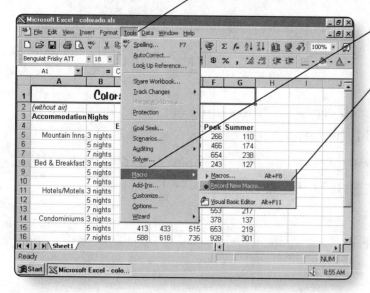

2. Click on **Macro**. A submenu will appear.

3. Click on **Record New Macro**. The Record Macro dialog box will open.

TIP

If you make mistakes, it is best just to delete your macro and start again. See the section, "Deleting Macros," for help.

4. **Type** a **name** for your macro in the Macro name: text box. It's not a good idea to accept the default name "Macro1" as it will be difficult to remember what Macro1 does if you create several macros.

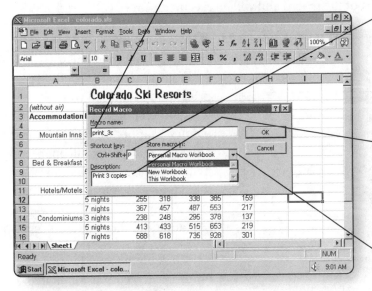

5. **Type** a **letter** in the Shortcut key: text box for the shortcut key for your macro. You can press the Shift key as you type the letter and more options will appear.

6. **Type** a **description** for your macro in the Description: text box. The description will appear in the Macro dialog box when you run the macro.

7. **Click** on the **down arrow** (▼) to the right of Store macro in:. A drop-down menu will appear.

8. **Click** on **Personal Macro Workbook**, **New Workbook**, or **This Workbook** to store your macro. Personal Macro Workbook is the best solution as you will probably want to have this macro available for use with all your worksheets.

9. **Click** on **OK**. The macro will be saved.

In addition, the Stop Recording toolbar will appear on your screen. If it doesn't, see the section, "Opening the Stop Recording Toolbar." From now until you click on the Stop Recording button, everything you do in Excel is recorded as part of the macro and will be executed.

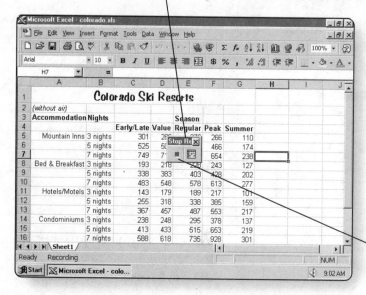

10. **Perform steps** you want to record for your macro. For example, to record a macro that prints three copies of your worksheet, click on File. The File menu will appear. Click on Print. The Print dialog box will open. In the Number of Copies: text box, change the number to 3 with the up and down arrows (⬍), and then click on OK.

11. Click on the **Stop Recording button**, when you've completed the tasks you want to record. The macro will be saved.

Opening the Stop Recording Toolbar

If the Stop Recording toolbar doesn't open, it could have been closed during a previous session.

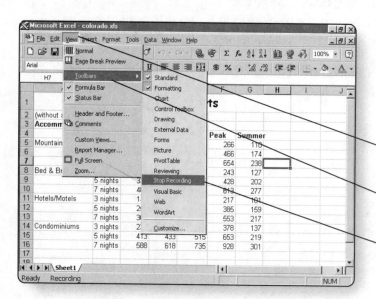

1. Click on **View**. The View menu will appear.

2. Click on **Toolbars**. A submenu will appear.

3. Click on **Stop Recording** to put a ✔. The Stop Recording toolbar will appear.

NOTE

You can use the same name for your macro. When Excel prompts you to replace the macro because the name already exists, click on Yes. This means the macro you are now creating is replacing the macro that recorded you opening the Stop Recording toolbar.

4. **Click** on the **Stop Recording button**.

5. **Repeat** the **steps** from "Recording and Naming Your Macro" starting with step 1 to re-record your macro.

RUNNING YOUR MACRO

If you saved the macro in your Personal Macro Workbook, it is available in every worksheet you create. If not you must be in the correct worksheet for your macro to work. To run your macro, you can:

1a. **Press** the **shortcut key** you assigned for the macro. The macro will run. For example, press the Ctrl, Shift, and P keys at the same time.

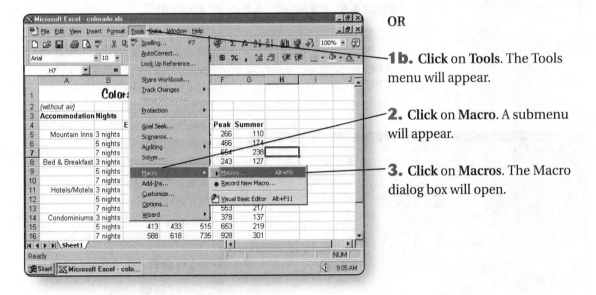

OR

1b. **Click** on **Tools**. The Tools menu will appear.

2. **Click** on **Macro**. A submenu will appear.

3. **Click** on **Macros**. The Macro dialog box will open.

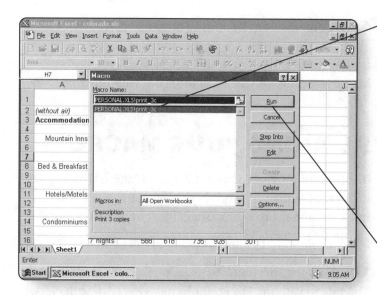

4. **Click** on the **name** of the macro you want to run. The name will be highlighted.

NOTE

If you added a description when you created the macro, it will appear in the Description box.

5. **Click** on **Run**. The macro will run.

DELETING MACROS

As stated previously, macros are either stored with a worksheet or in your Personal Macro Workbook. You need to have the appropriate worksheet or workbook open to delete a macro. If you saved your macro with a specific worksheet, simply open the worksheet. If you saved it with the Personal Macro Workbook, which is automatically opened when you start Excel, you need to unhide it.

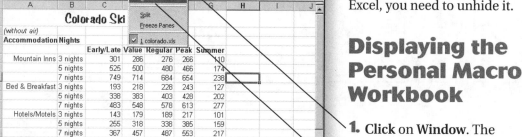

Displaying the Personal Macro Workbook

1. **Click** on **Window**. The Window menu will appear.

2. **Click** on **Unhide**. The Unhide dialog box will open.

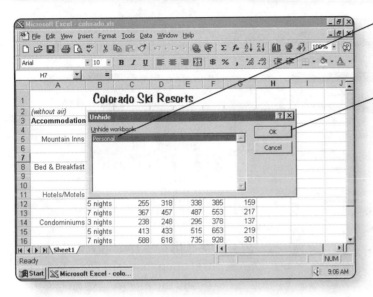

3. **Click** on **Personal** in the Unhide workbook: text box. The item will be highlighted.

4. **Click** on **OK**. The workbook will open.

Deleting a Macro with a Workbook or Worksheet Open

1. **Click** on **Tools**. The Tools menu will appear.

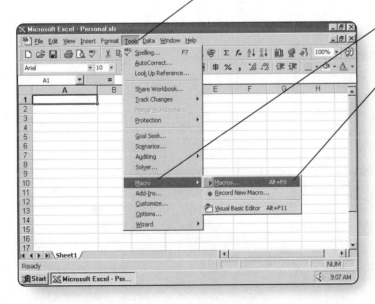

2. **Click** on **Macro**. A submenu will appear.

3. **Click** on **Macros**. The Macro dialog box will open.

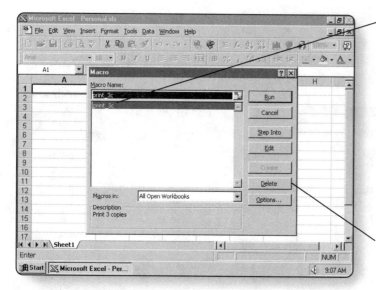

4. Click on the **macro** you want to delete. The name will be highlighted.

TIP

Check the description at the bottom of the Macro dialog box so that you are sure you're deleting the correct macro.

5. Click on **Delete**. A dialog box will open that asks if you want to delete the macro.

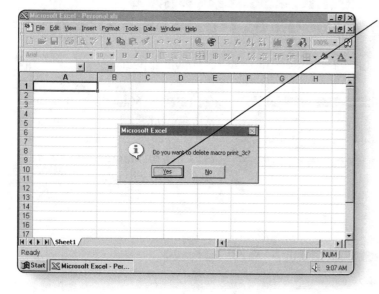

6. Click on **Yes**. The macro will be deleted.

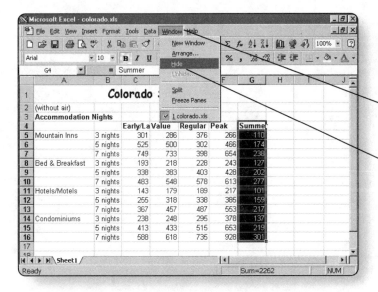

Hiding the Personal Macro Workbook

1. **Click** on **Window**. The Window menu will appear.

2. **Click** on **Hide**. The workbook will be hidden.

NOTE

If you don't hide the Personal Macro Workbook while you're working in Excel, the next time you open the program it will be hidden.

9 Working with Data

Excel can be used not only to perform calculations but also to store data which you can then sort and search to find information and make decisions. In this chapter, you'll learn how to:

✦ Sort data by rows and columns

✦ Search for information that meets specific criteria

✦ Protect your data

SORTING DATA

If you enter a large amount of data into a worksheet it may be easier to find information you need by sorting your data. You can easily sort data in Excel either alphabetically or numerically, in ascending or descending order.

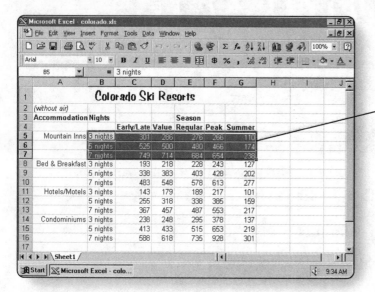

Sorting the Order of Rows in a Range

1. **Click** and **drag** the **mouse arrow** to highlight the cells of the range you want to sort. Be sure to select all the data associated with the row labels you've selected. If you don't select all of the relevant data, you may scramble your worksheet.

TIP
If you think you may not have included all the data after you've sorted your worksheet, click on Undo.

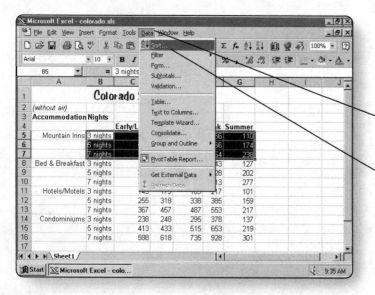

2. **Click** on **Data**. The Data menu will appear.

3. **Click** on **Sort**. The Sort dialog box will open.

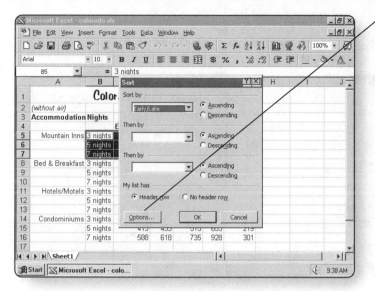

4. **Click** on **Options**. The Sort Options dialog box will open.

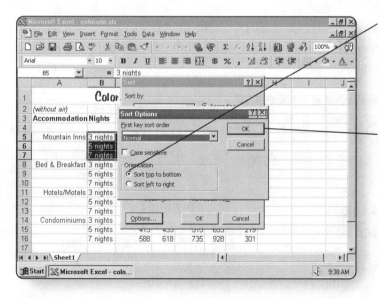

5. **Click** on **Sort top to bottom** in the Orientation box. Sort top to bottom sorts rows, whereas Sort left to right rearranges columns.

6. **Click** on **OK**. The Sort dialog box will appear.

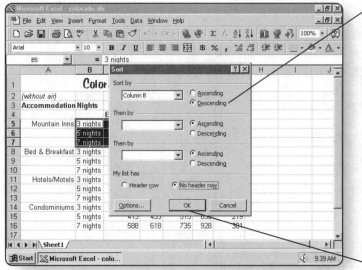

7. Click on **Descending** in the Sort by box. Ascending sorts alphabetically, A through Z or numerically, smallest to largest. Descending is the opposite; Z through A and largest to smallest.

NOTE

To sort with the smaller number on top, click on Ascending in step 7.

8. Click on **OK**. The Sort dialog box will close.

The data will be sorted numerically from largest to smallest. In this example, the data appears with 7 nights at the top and 3 nights at the bottom.

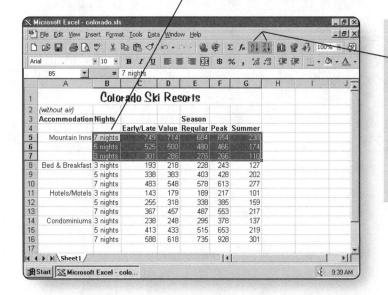

TIP

You can also sort using the Sort Ascending and Sort Descending toolbar buttons. These sort the selected items in order alphabetically or numerically using the column that contains the insertion point.

Sorting the Order of Columns in a Range

1. **Click** and **drag** the **mouse arrow** to highlight the cells of the range you want to sort. Be sure to include all the data applicable to the column heads in the range.

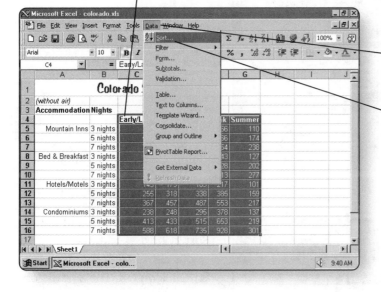

2. **Click** on **Data**. The Data menu will appear.

3. **Click** on **Sort**. The Sort dialog box will open.

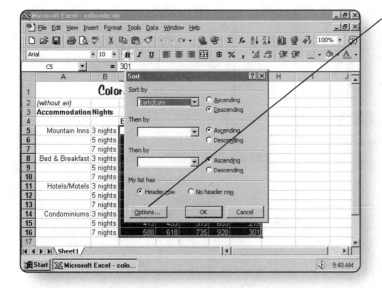

4. **Click** on **Options**. The Sort Options dialog box will open.

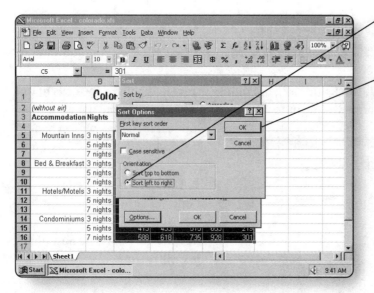

5. Click on **Sort left to right** in the Orientation box.

6. Click on **OK**. The Sort dialog box will appear.

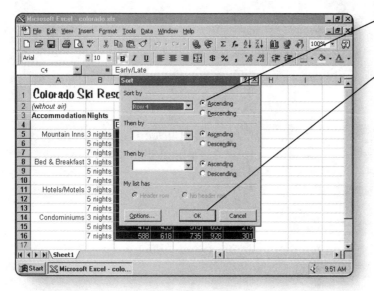

7. Click on **Ascending** in the Sort by box.

8. Click on **OK**. The Sort dialog box will close.

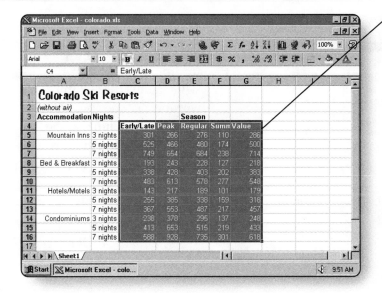

The data will appear sorted alphabetically by column head, left to right.

FILTERING DATA

You can search for data using the Filter command to select information that meets criteria of your choosing. For example, you can set up a filter that will search through accommodation prices in a worksheet and pull up all accommodations during the peak season that are less than $400.

1. Click on the **column head** that you want to use in your search. The cell will be highlighted.

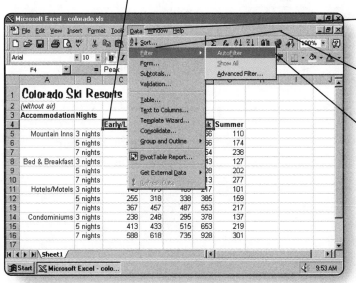

2. Click on **Data**. The Data menu will appear.

3. Click on **Filter**. A submenu will appear.

4. Click on **AutoFilter**. AutoFilter arrows will appear next to the column heads.

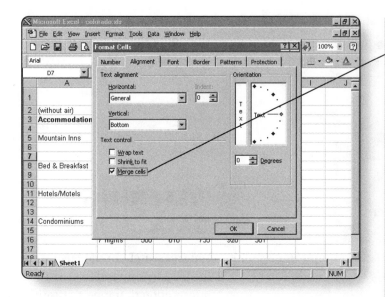

If you have a merged cell in the first row of your worksheet, across the columns, you will only get one AutoFilter arrow in the column at the far right. Click on Format, and then Cells. The Format Cells dialog box will appear. Click on the Alignment tab. Finally, click on Merge Cells in the Text Control box to put a ✔ next to it. The merge format will be removed.

In this example, the criteria are for peak season, and accommodations under $400.

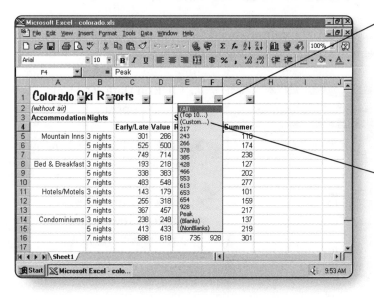

5. **Click** on the **down arrow** (▼) in the column for "Peak." All the entries in the Peak column will appear in the drop-down list. You can select any of the options in the list to see only those rows in the worksheet.

6. **Click** on **Custom**. A criterion for selecting rows in the worksheet will be set up. The Custom AutoFilter dialog box will open.

7. **Click** on the **down arrow** (▼) next to "equals." A drop-down list will appear.

8. **Click** on **is less than**. Your selection will be highlighted.

9. **Tab** to the **next text box** to the right and **type $400**.

10. **Click** on **OK**.

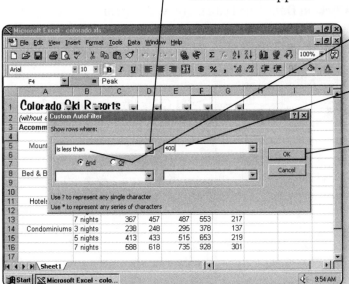

TIP

You can continue to refine your requirements in the Custom AutoFilter dialog box. For example, you could search for less than $400 and more than $350, using "And" with the additional text boxes.

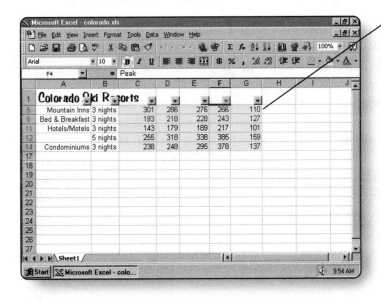

The worksheet will now only show accommodations that meet the criteria of being less than $400 in the peak season.

Turning AutoFilter Off

1. Click on **Data**. The Data menu will appear.

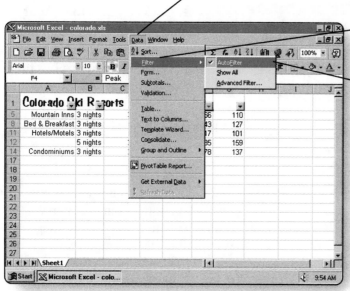

2. Click on **Filter**. A submenu will appear.

3. Click on **AutoFilter**. The worksheet will appear as it was before the search.

PROTECTING YOUR DATA

If you've invested a great deal of time and effort constructing a worksheet or workbook you want to be sure no one can either by accident, or worse, intentionally, make unauthorized changes to your data. You can protect your work at the worksheet level by allowing others to view but not edit the sheet without a password. At the workbook level, you can prevent worksheets from being moved, hidden, renamed, and windows being moved, resized, hidden, or closed. Be aware that if you lose the password you cannot gain access to the files, data, or options you've password protected. You should always write down the password and keep it in a secure place.

Protecting Your Worksheet

You can protect the integrity of the data in your worksheet by setting up password protection.

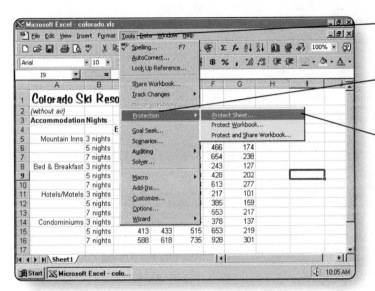

1. **Click** on **Tools**. The Tools menu will appear.

2. **Click** on **Protection**. A submenu will appear.

3. **Click** on **Protect Sheet**. The Protect Sheet dialog box will open.

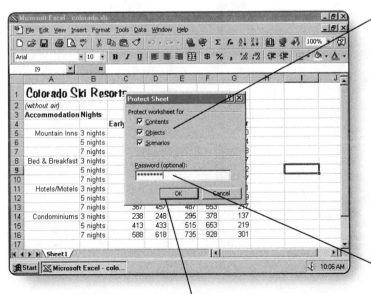

4. **Click** on **Contents**, **Objects**, and **Scenarios** under Protect worksheet for. A ✔ will appear next to each item.

TIP

Objects include items such as charts, while scenarios are named sets of values you can use to substitute in a worksheet model.

5. **Type** a **password**.

6. **Click** on **OK**. The Confirm Password dialog box will open.

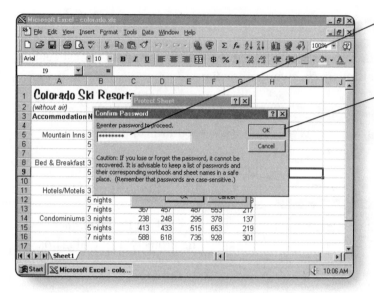

7. **Type** the **password** again to ensure you typed it correctly the first time.

8. **Click** on **OK**. The Confirm Password dialog box will close.

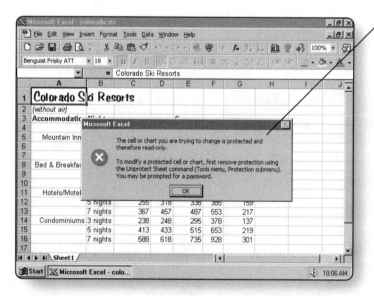

The worksheet can be opened and viewed, but if someone tries to change the data, a prompt will be displayed that says the worksheet is password protected. To remove the protection, you must enter a password first. Without the password, changes cannot be made.

Removing Password Protection from Worksheets

1. **Click** on **Tools**. The Tools menu will appear.

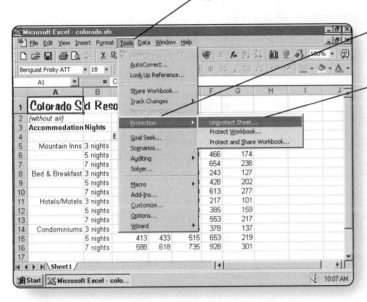

2. **Click** on **Protection**. A submenu will appear.

3. **Click** on **Unprotect Sheet**. The Unprotect Sheet dialog box will open.

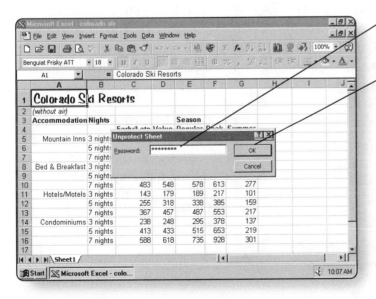

4. **Type** the **password** in the Password: text box.

5. **Click** on **OK**. The worksheet will be unprotected.

Protecting Your Workbook

You can also protect your worksheets at the workbook or file level.

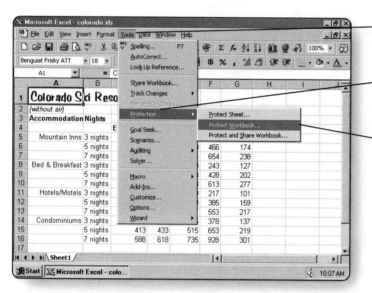

1. Click on **Tools**. The Tools menu will appear.

2. Click on **Protection**. A submenu will appear.

3. Click on **Protect Workbook**. The Protect Workbook dialog box will open.

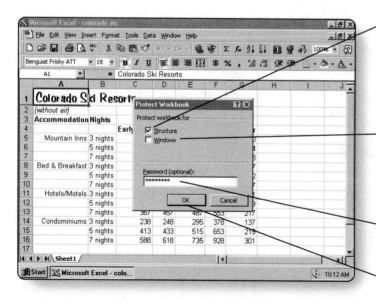

4. Click on **Structure** to put a ✔ next to it. This will prevent the worksheets from being moved, hidden, renamed, or new sheets from being added.

5. Click on **Windows** to put a ✔ next to it. This will prevent windows from being moved, resized, hidden, or closed.

6. Type a **password** in the Password text box.

7. Click on **OK**. The Confirm Password dialog box will open.

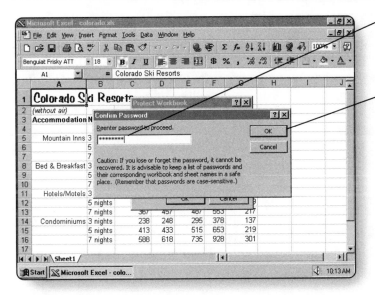

8. **Type** the **password** again to ensure you typed it correctly the first time.

9. **Click** on **OK**. Now all commands related to modifying the structure of the workbook or the windows in the workbook will be unavailable (dimmed on the menus) as long as the protection is on.

Removing Password Protection from Workbooks

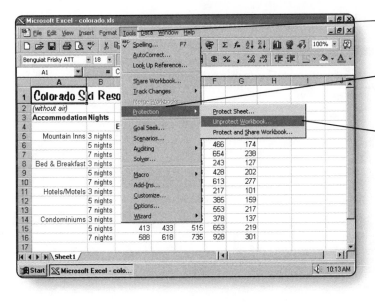

1. **Click** on **Tools**. The Tools menu will appear.

2. **Click** on **Protection**. A submenu will appear.

3. **Click** on **Unprotect Workbook**. The Unprotect Workbook dialog box will open.

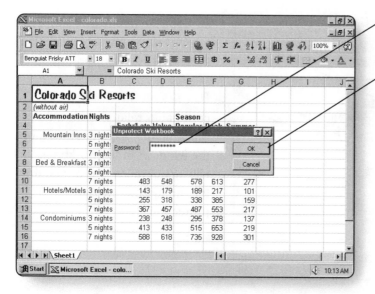

4. **Type** the **password** in the Password: text box.

5. **Click** on **OK**. The workbook will be unprotected.

Preventing Your Workbook from Being Opened

1. **Click** on **File**. The File menu will appear.

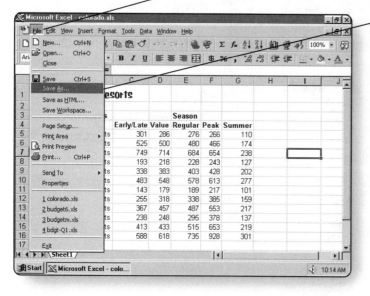

2. **Click** on **Save As**. The Save As dialog box will open.

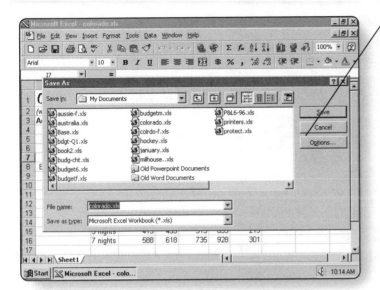

3. **Click** on **Options**. The Save Options dialog box will open.

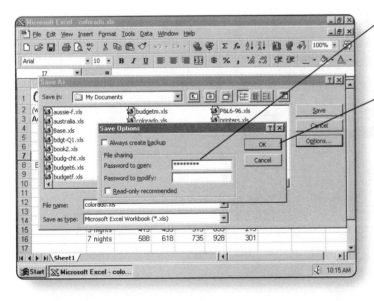

4. **Type** a **password** in the Password to open: text box. Passwords are case-sensitive.

5. **Click** on **OK**. The Confirm Password dialog box will open.

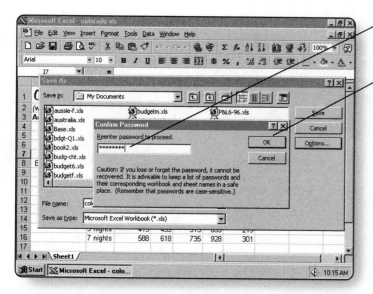

6. Type the **password** again in the Reenter password... text box.

7. Click on **OK**. The Save As dialog box will appear.

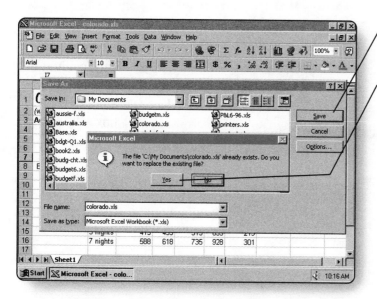

8. Click on **Save**. A prompt will appear.

9. Click on **Yes**. The existing workbook will be replaced.

10 Working with Wizards and Templates

Both wizards and templates make working with Excel much easier. Wizards ask you for relevant information and then perform a task for you, whereas templates are built-in forms which enable you to produce professional-looking documents like invoices with just a few keystrokes. In this chapter, you'll learn how to:

✦ Use a wizard

✦ Open a template

✦ Customize a template

✦ Create a document using a template

USING A WIZARD

Wizards help you perform difficult tasks by prompting you for required information and then performing a task for you. There are several Excel wizards available to you. The Lookup Wizard helps you write a formula that finds the value at the intersection of a row and column. The File Conversion Wizard helps you convert files created in other programs, like Lotus 1-2-3, so that you can use them in Excel. The Web Form Wizard configures your worksheet so it can be used as a Web form to submit information to a database.

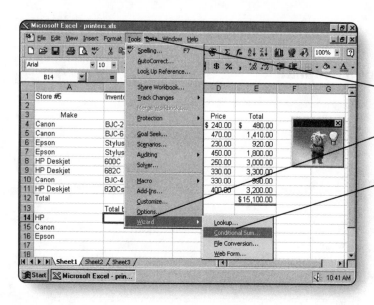

The Conditional Sum Wizard

In this example, you'll learn about the Conditional Sum Wizard. You can use this wizard to add numbers (the numbers that represent the value of all the HP printers) that meet particular criteria.

1. Click on **Tools**. The Tools menu will appear.

2. Click on **Wizard**. A submenu will appear.

3. Click on **Conditional Sum**. The Conditional Sum Wizard – Step 1 of 4 dialog box will open. It will ask for a list that "contains the values to sum, including the column labels."

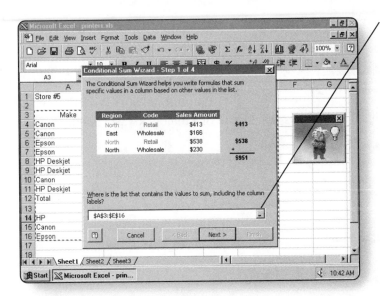

4. Click on the **Collapse Dialog button**. You return to the worksheet.

5. Click and drag the **mouse arrow** across the range which contains the data you want to sum. The cells will be highlighted. Don't forget to include the labels at the top of the rows.

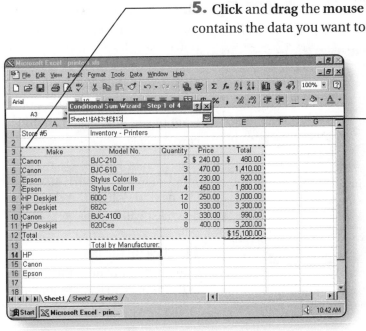

6. Click on the **Expand Dialog button** to return to the Wizard. The Step 1 dialog box will reappear.

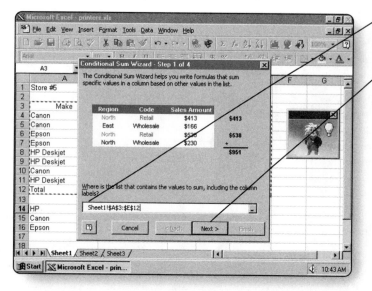

The range you selected will be entered in the dialog box.

7. **Click** on **Next**. The Conditional Sum Wizard – Step 2 of 4 dialog box will open.

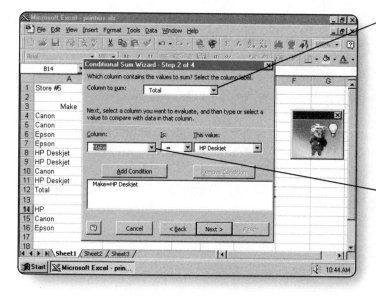

8. **Click** on the **down arrow** (▼) next to Column to sum:. A drop-down list will appear.

9. **Click** on the **label** for the column where the numbers you want to add are located, in this case, "Total."

10. **Click** on the **down arrow** (▼) next to Column:. A drop-down list will appear.

11. **Click** on the **label** for the column that includes the name of the items you want to include, in this case, "Make."

The Is: drop-down list enables you to select an operator. In this case, the equal sign is the default.

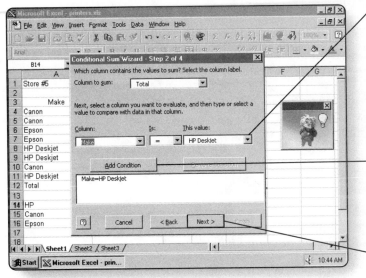

12. Click on the **down arrow** (▼) next to This value:. A drop-down list will appear.

13. Click on the **label** for the items you want to add, in this case, "HP Deskjet."

14. Click on **Add Condition** and check that the statement that appears in the text box is what you want to do.

15. Click on **Next**. The Conditional Sum Wizard – Step 3 of 4 dialog box will open.

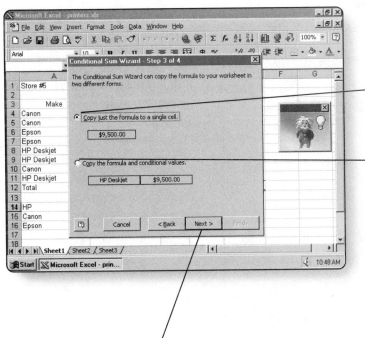

16. Click on one of the two copying **options**:

✦ Click on **Copy just the formula to a single cell**.

OR

✦ Click on **Copy the formula and conditional values**.

NOTE

Click on the formula and the conditional value option if you will want to sum different values within the same column later.

17. Click on **Next**. The Conditional Sum Wizard – Step 4 of 4 dialog box will open.

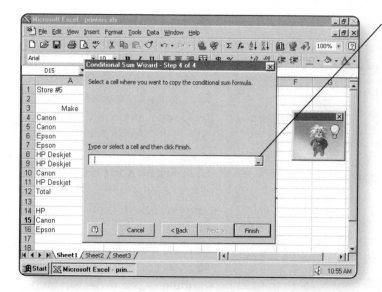

18. Click on the **Collapse Dialog button** to return to the worksheet. The dialog box will shrink.

19. Click in the **cell** where you want the total to appear. The cell will be highlighted.

20. Click on the **Expand Dialog button** to return to the wizard. The dialog box will reappear.

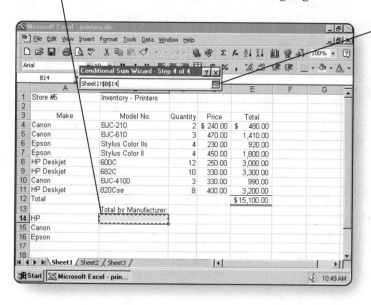

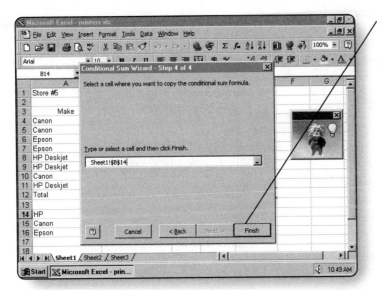

21. Click on **Finish**. The dialog box will close.

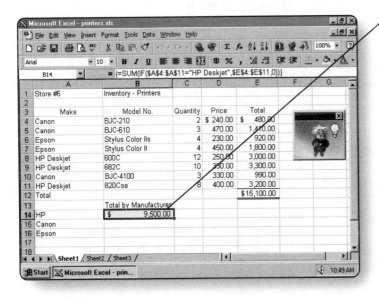

The result will appear in the selected cell.

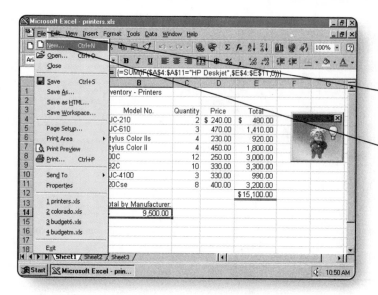

OPENING A TEMPLATE

1. **Click** on **File**. The File menu will appear.

2. **Click** on **New**. The New dialog box will open.

3. **Click** on the **Spreadsheet Solutions tab**. The tab will come to the front.

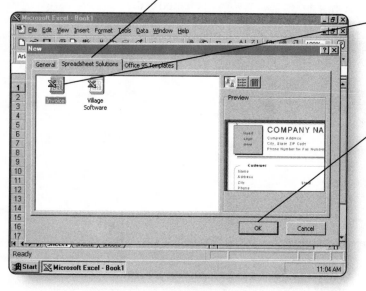

4. **Click** on the **Invoice icon**. The icon will be highlighted. You will be able to see a small portion of the Invoice template in the Preview box as well.

5. **Click** on **OK**. The macro warning dialog box will appear. It explains that macros may contain viruses and that you can disable the macros if you're not sure if the workbook template is from a trusted source.

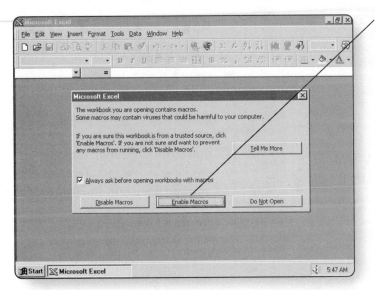

6. **Click** on **Enable Macros**. Since this template came with the Excel 97 software, it should be safe.

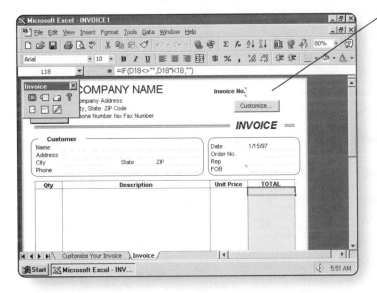

The Invoice template will open. It doesn't look like a worksheet, but it is. It has cells and a Formula bar.

At this point you can customize the template, print it to fill it out by hand, or fill it out onscreen and print it. The next section explains how to customize the Invoice template.

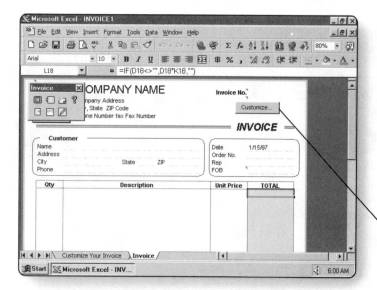

CUSTOMIZING YOUR TEMPLATE

You can add your company name, address, phone number, and so on to your invoice and save it as a new template, which you can use again and again.

1. **Click** on **Customize** to enter your personal information. The Customize Your Invoice worksheet will appear.

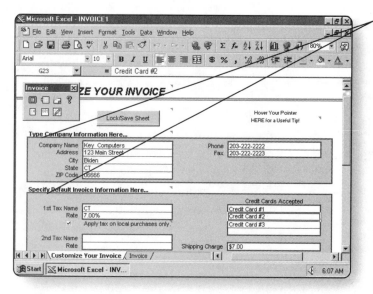

You can now replace the boilerplate text in the form. Enter all the information that you want to appear on your invoices such as your company name, address, phone numbers, states and purchase tax rates, credit cards, if appropriate, and shipping charges.

2. **Press** the **Enter key** or **click** in each **text box** to move between entries.

TIP

Move the pointer over the red triangles to get helpful information.

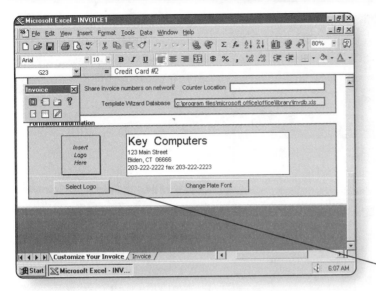

Adding a Logo

Adding a company logo is optional. If you don't want to add a logo, do not follow the steps below. The Insert Logo Here box will not print on your invoice.

1. **Scroll** to the **bottom** of the **Customize Your Invoice worksheet** to the Formatted Information area.

2. **Click** on **Select Logo**. The Insert Picture dialog box will open.

3. **Locate** the **graphic** you want to use. You'll need to look for a folder that contains graphic files. The clip art files that came with Microsoft Office are probably in a directory called "Clipart" inside the Microsoft Office folder.

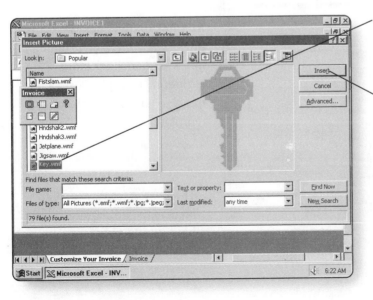

4. **Click** on the **filename** of the graphic you want to use. The filename will be highlighted.

5. **Click** on **Insert**. The logo will appear in the Formatted Information box.

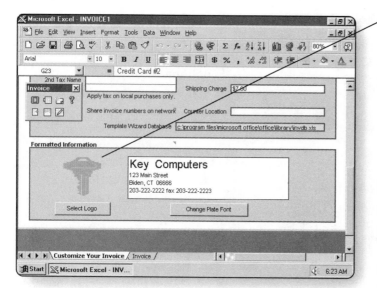

The logo and address will appear at the top of all your invoices as if you were using preprinted letterhead.

Saving the Customized Invoice Template

Once you've finished customizing your invoice template, you'll want to save it so you can use it again and again.

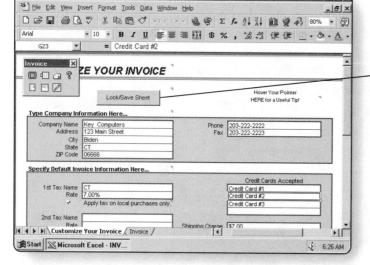

1. **Scroll** to the **top** of the **Customize Your Invoice worksheet**.

2. **Click** on the **Lock/Save Sheet button**. The Lock/Save dialog box will open. Lock stops accidental changes from being made to your customized template.

NOTE

The Lock/Save button will change to Unlock after you have locked your template. You can click on this button at a later date to make changes.

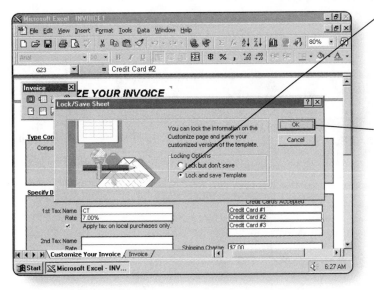

3. **Click** on **Lock and save Template**. By selecting Lock and save Template, you are creating your own version of the template for future use.

4. **Click** on **OK**. The Save Template dialog box will open.

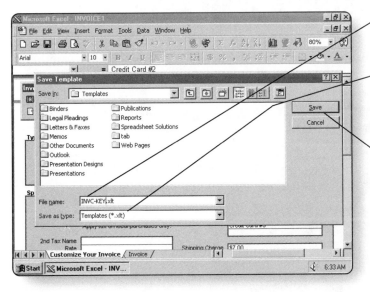

5. **Type** a **name** for your invoice in the File name: text box.

6. **Make sure Templates** is selected in the Save as type: text box.

7. **Click** on **Save**. A dialog box will open.

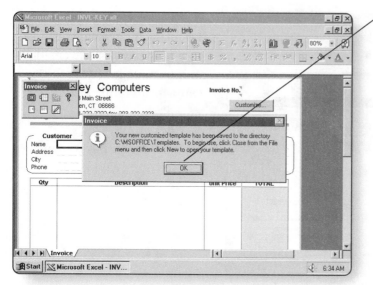

8. **Click** on **OK**. The new customized template will be saved. You can use it now, or close and open it again when you need it. An icon for your customized template file should appear on the General tab of the New dialog box.

USING A TEMPLATE

This section shows you how to use a template to create a document. The steps are the same for any template whether it's built-in or a customized template.

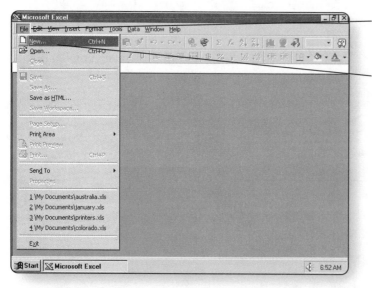

1. **Click** on **File**. The File menu will appear.

2. **Click** on **New**. The New dialog box will open.

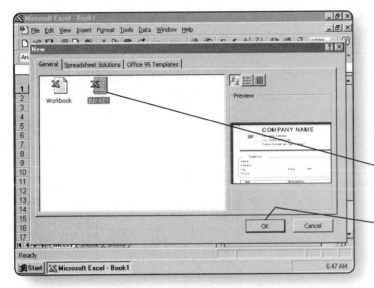

3. **Click** on the **tab** where the template icon you want to use is located. As a general rule, the built-in templates are on the Spreadsheets Solution tab and the custom templates are on the General tab.

4. **Click** on the **template icon**. The icon will be highlighted.

5. **Click** on **OK**. The template will appear.

NOTE

If the macro warning message appears again, click on Enable Macros.

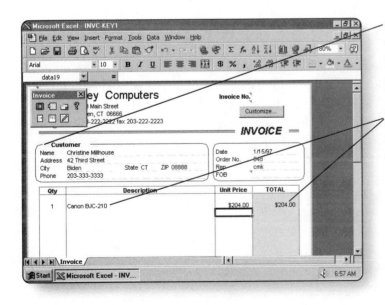

6. **Type** the **information** you want to appear in the template. In this example, you enter Customer information.

7. **Type** the **items** to be invoiced. You may need to scroll down the screen.

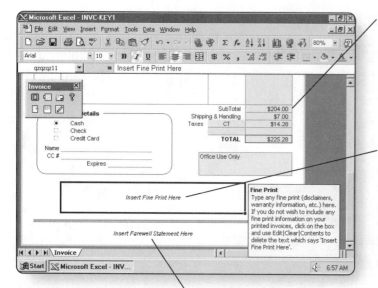

Notice that the template contains the formulas and functions to calculate all the totals including shipping and handling, and taxes. These items are added automatically.

Insert Fine Print Here can be selected and replaced with information for the customer, such as a returns policy or warranties, or it can be deleted by clicking on Edit and then Clear.

Similarly, Insert Farewell Statement Here can be selected and replaced with text such as a company slogan or mission statement, or it can be deleted by clicking on Edit and then Clear.

Saving a Customized Template

You have a couple of choices when you change a new document that you've based on a template. You can simply save it as you would any other document; because it was opened as a document based on a template, it will simply be saved as a document automatically. Or, you can save it as a template with a new name.

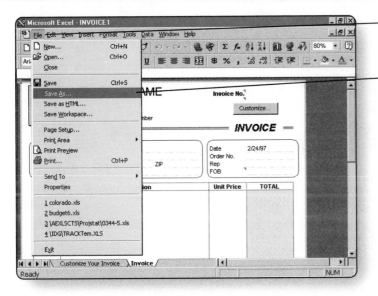

1. Click on **File**. The File menu will appear.

2. Click on **Save As**. The Save As dialog box will open.

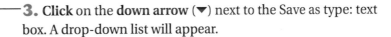

3. Click on the **down arrow** (▼) next to the Save as type: text box. A drop-down list will appear.

4. Click on the **Template (*.xlt)** file type. It will be selected.

5. Type a **name** for the file in the File name: text box.

6. Click on Save. The file will be saved as a template and be available from the New dialog box as a template.

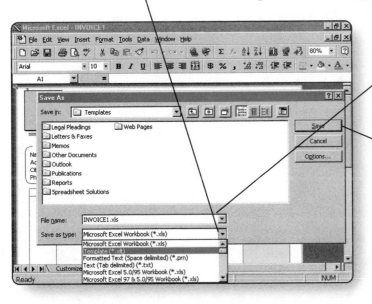

11 Exploring Printing Options

Although you can send your worksheets directly to paper by clicking on File, and then Print, as described in Chapter 3, "Saving, Printing, and Exiting Excel," there are other options available. These options will not only make your documents look more professional but will also save you time and money by letting you see exactly what you're going to print, before you use any paper. In this chapter, you'll learn how to:

+ Set paper size, paper orientation, and margins

+ Add headers and footers

+ Select rows and columns to print on every page

+ Select the print area

+ Set page breaks

+ Preview your document

SETTING PAPER SIZE AND ORIENTATION

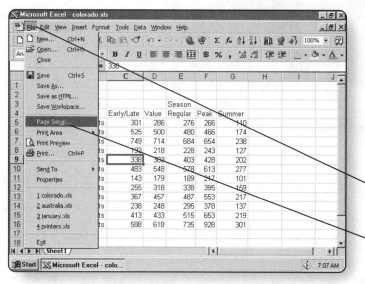

Unlike letters which are always printed using Portrait orientation, worksheets, depending on their size, may look better printed using Landscape orientation. You'll need to make decisions about how your printouts will look.

1. **Click** on **File**. The File menu will appear.

2. **Click** on **Page Setup**. The Page Setup dialog box will open.

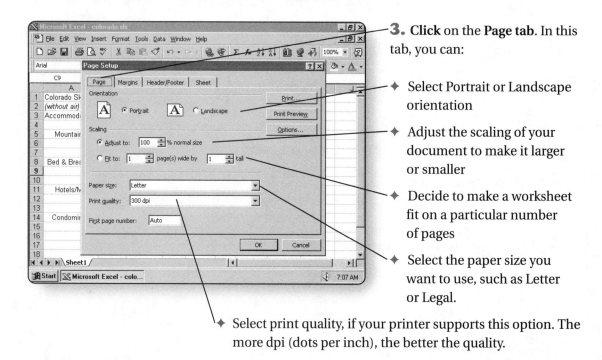

3. **Click** on the **Page tab**. In this tab, you can:

✦ Select Portrait or Landscape orientation

✦ Adjust the scaling of your document to make it larger or smaller

✦ Decide to make a worksheet fit on a particular number of pages

✦ Select the paper size you want to use, such as Letter or Legal.

✦ Select print quality, if your printer supports this option. The more dpi (dots per inch), the better the quality.

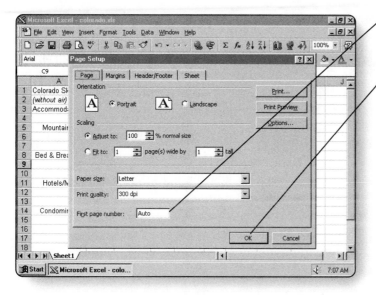

◆ Select the first page number to print, if you don't want to start at 1.

4a. **Click** on **OK**. Your selections will be saved and the Page Setup dialog box will close.

OR

4b. **Click** on **another tab** to get more options.

SETTING MARGINS

To adjust your margins, click on File, and then Page Setup to open the Page Setup dialog box, if it's not already open.

1. **Click** on the **Margins tab**. In this tab, you can:

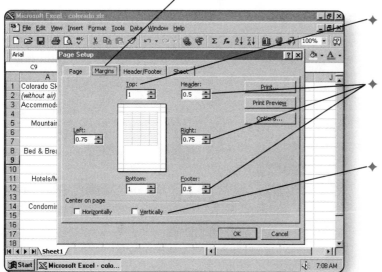

◆ Adjust the top, bottom, left, and right margins using the up and down arrows (◆).

◆ Adjust where the header and footer appear on a page by clicking on the up and down arrows (◆).

◆ Select to center a document either horizontally, vertically, or both.

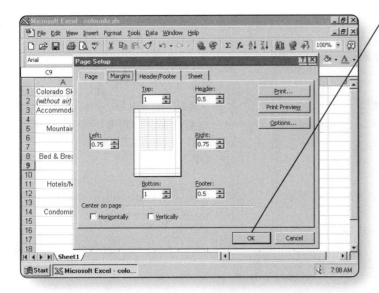

2a. Click on **OK**. Your selections will be saved and the Page Setup dialog box will close.

OR

2b. Click on **another tab** to get more options.

ADDING HEADERS AND FOOTERS

Headers and footers are simply text which appears either at the top (header) or bottom (footer) of every page. The types of information typically included in headers and footers are report titles, dates, page numbers, or filenames.

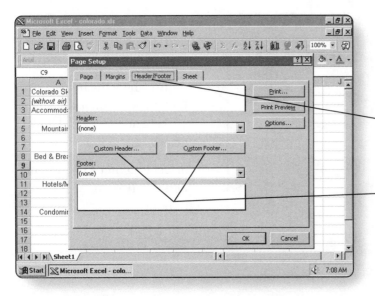

To add header and footers, click on File, and then Page Setup to open the Page Setup dialog box, if it's not already open.

1. Click on the **Header/Footer tab**. The tab will come to the front.

2. Click on **Custom Header** or **Custom Footer**. The Header or Footer dialog box will open.

3. **Click** in the **Left**, **Center**, or **Right section text box**. This determines where the text you insert will appear; left, right, or centered on the printed page.

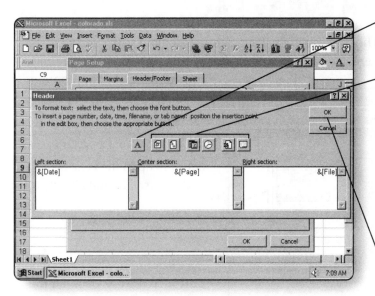

4. **Click** on the **A button** to select a new font for your text.

5. **Insert** a **page number**, **date**, **time**, **filename**, or **tab name** in a text box by clicking on the appropriate button.

6. **Type** the **text** that you want to appear in the header or footer in the appropriate text box.

7. **Click** on **OK**. The Header/Footer tab will reappear.

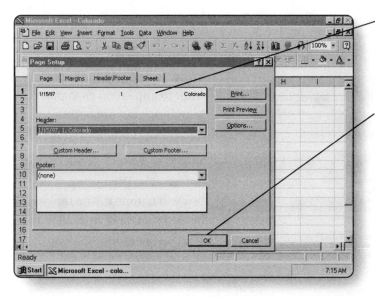

Notice that you will see a preview of how the header or footer will appear in the Header/Footer tab.

8a. **Click** on **OK**. Your selections will be saved and the Page Setup dialog box will close.

OR

8b. **Click** on **another tab** to get more options.

SELECTING ROWS AND COLUMNS TO APPEAR ON EVERY PAGE

The final tab in the Page Setup dialog box is the Sheet tab. From here you can make a number of choices including selecting rows or columns, that contain headings or labels, to repeat on every page.

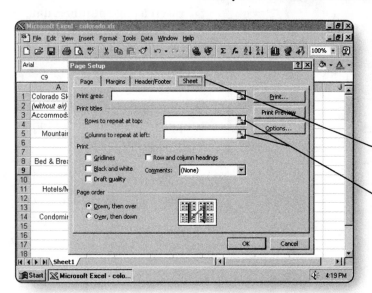

First, click on File, and then Page Setup to open the Page Setup dialog box, if it's not already open.

1. **Click** on the **Sheet tab**. The tab will come to the front.

2. **Click** on the **Collapse Dialog button** at the end of either the Rows to repeat at top: or Columns to repeat at left: text box. The Page Setup dialog box will shrink to reveal the worksheet.

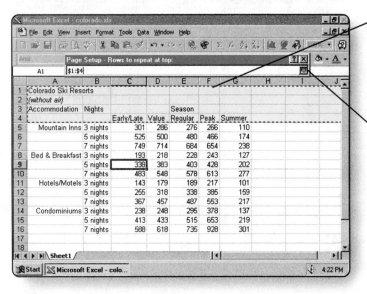

3. **Click** and **drag** the **mouse arrow** to select the cells you want to appear on each page. Marching ants will appear around the highlighted cells.

4. **Click** on the **Expand Dialog button**. The Page Setup dialog box will reappear. The range will be automatically entered in the correct Print titles text box.

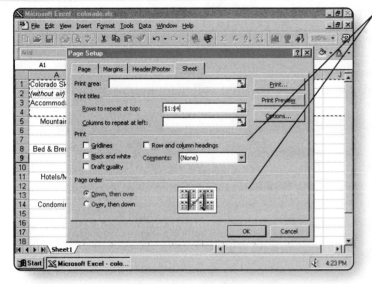

Other options in the Sheet tab you can select are:

◆ **Gridlines.** Your printout will have the same grid as your worksheet does on the screen. If you don't select this option, there are no lines separating the rows and columns on the printout, even though you see them on the screen.

◆ **Black and white.** This will save the ink in your color printing cartridge, if you have one. Color cartridges are usually more expensive than black and white.

◆ **Draft quality.** Printing in draft quality is quicker, although the printout will not be quite as sharp.

◆ **Row and column headings.** Select row and column headings to print column letters and row numbers.

◆ **Comments.** You can choose to not print your comments by clicking on (None) from the drop-down list. You can also select to either print your comments at the end of the worksheet or as displayed on the sheet.

◆ **Page order.** If your worksheet is both wider and longer than a single page, you can also choose whether to print pages down the worksheet before going across, or whether to go across first and then down.

5a. Click on **OK**. Your selections will be saved and the Page Setup dialog box will close.

OR

5b. Click on **another tab** to get more options.

SETTING THE PRINT AREA

You may not want to print your entire worksheet. For example, you may have 12 months of data in the worksheet and you only want to print the information for the current month.

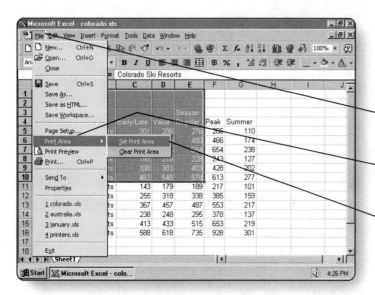

1. **Click** and **drag** with the **mouse arrow** over the area in the worksheet you want to print. The cells will be highlighted.

2. **Click** on **File**. The File menu will appear.

3. **Click** on **Print Area**. A submenu will appear.

4. **Click** on **Set Print Area**. The menu will disappear and you will see a dotted line around the area you've selected. When you print now, only the Print Area will be printed.

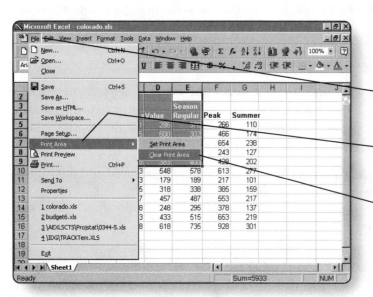

Clearing the Print Area

1. **Click** on **File**. The File menu will appear.

2. **Click** on **Print Area**. A submenu will appear.

3. **Click** on **Clear Print Area**. The area will be cleared.

PREVIEWING YOUR WORKSHEET

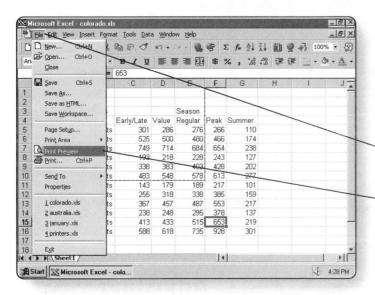

You'll probably save yourself a lot of paper if you always preview your worksheet to see what it looks like and check the margins before sending it to the printer.

1. **Click** on **File**. The File menu will appear.

2. **Click** on **Print Preview**. The print preview window will open.

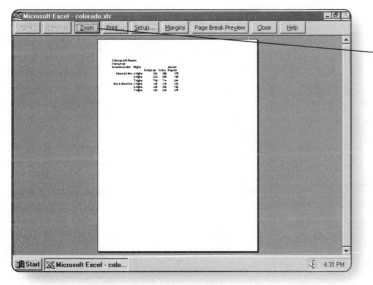

Zooming

1. **Click** on the **Zoom button** to zoom to a closer view of your worksheet. The worksheet will be magnified.

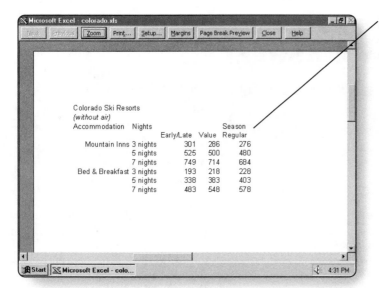

2. Click on **Zoom** again. The worksheet will shrink.

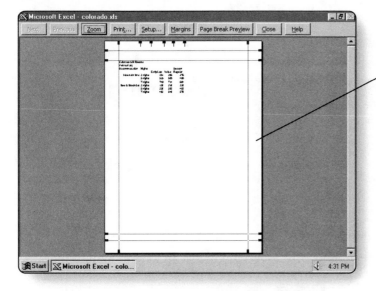

Adjusting Margins

1. Click on the **Margin button**. The margin settings, columns, and header and footer areas of your worksheet will be revealed.

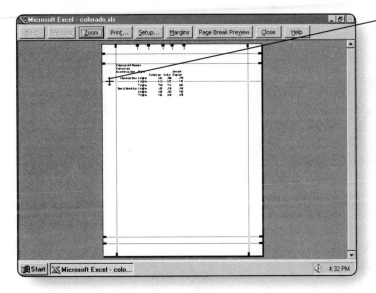

2. **Move** the **mouse arrow** over a margin line until it changes to a double-headed arrow.

3. **Press** and **hold** the **mouse button** as you **drag** the margin in or out, or up or down.

4. **Release** the **mouse button**. The new setting will take effect.

Previewing Page Breaks

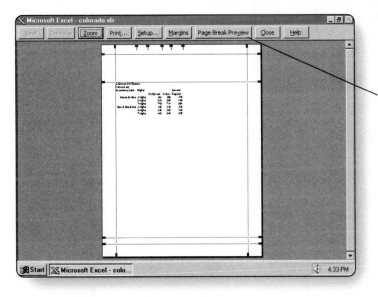

Page Breaks are inserted by Excel to divide large worksheets into pages.

1. **Click** on **Page Break Preview**. The Welcome to Page Break Preview dialog box will open.

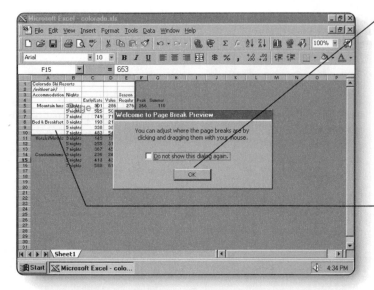

2. Click on **OK**. In the worksheet, you will see where Excel has inserted page breaks either because it knows it can't fit more information on a page or because you selected a particular page range. You can move page breaks, to get a better grouping of rows on pages.

3. Click on the **dotted line**. A double-headed arrow will appear.

4. Drag the **page break indicator** to a new position.

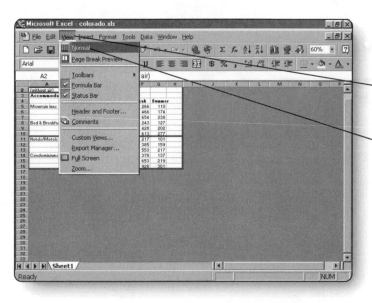

Closing Page Break Preview

1. Click on **View**. The View menu will appear.

2. Click on **Normal**. You will return to Normal view.

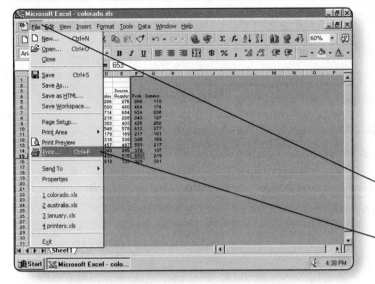

PRINTING YOUR WORKSHEET

Now that you've checked all your printing options, you are ready to print.

1. Click on **File**. The File menu will appear.

2. Click on **Print**. The Print dialog box will open.

3. Click on **OK**. The document will be printed.

Refer to Chapter 3, "Saving, Printing, and Exiting Excel," for more information about options in the Print dialog box.

PART II REVIEW QUESTIONS

1. In Excel, what is a range? *See "Selecting Cells" in Chapter 5.*

2. How can you quickly fill a range with a series of data? *See "Filling a Range" in Chapter 5.*

3. What role do formulas play in Excel? *See "Entering a Simple Calculation" in Chapter 6.*

4. In Excel, what are functions? *See "Using Built-In Functions" in Chapter 6.*

5. Why would you want to name a range? *See "Naming a Range" in Chapter 7.*

6. Why would you want to split an Excel window? *See "Splitting a Window" in Chapter 7.*

7. What is a macro? *See the introduction in Chapter 8.*

8. In Excel, how can you tell Excel to search for specific data rather than text? *See "Searching and Selecting Data" in Chapter 9.*

9. In Excel, what are the differences between wizards and templates? *See the introduction in Chapter 10.*

10. What feature can you use to see your worksheet before you print it? *See "Previewing Your Worksheet" in Chapter 11.*

PART III

Making Your Data Look Good

12 Formatting Text

You can make your worksheets easier to read and more interesting by formatting text effectively. You can use different fonts, change the alignment, add borders, lines, colors, and more! In this chapter, you'll learn how to:

✦ **Use AutoFormat**

✦ **Change the type and size of a font**

✦ **Use bold, italic, and underline styles**

✦ **Align your text**

✦ **Center a heading across your worksheet**

USING AUTOFORMAT

If you're not artistically-inclined, AutoFormat is a great tool for creating cool worksheets quickly and easily. AutoFormat allows you to choose from a number of professionally-designed formats which automatically add colors, fonts, lines, borders, and more to your worksheets.

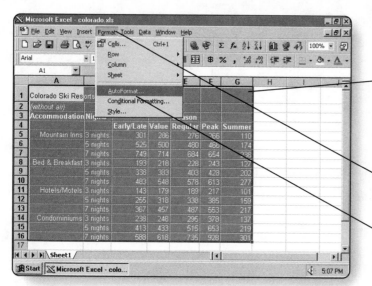

1. **Click** and **drag** with the **mouse arrow** across the cells you want to format. The cells will be highlighted.

2. **Click** on **Format**. The Format menu will appear.

3. **Click** on **AutoFormat**. The AutoFormat dialog box will open.

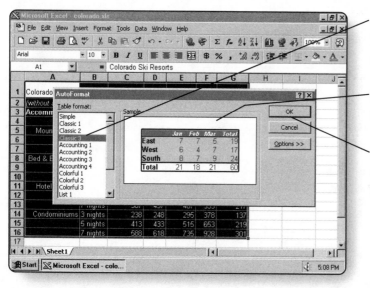

4. **Click** on a **selection** in the Table format: list. The selection will be highlighted.

5. **Preview** the **effect** in the Sample area.

6. **Click** on **OK** when you find an effect you like. The effect will be applied to the table.

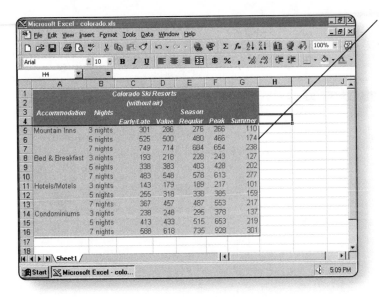

Depending on your selection, AutoFormat may have applied color, changed your fonts, applied italic or bold, and adjusted row heights.

Removing AutoFormat

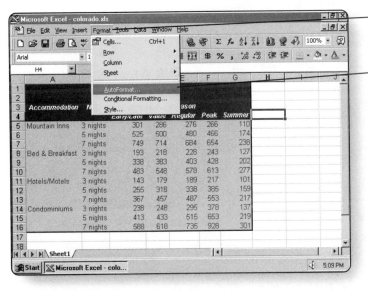

1. **Click** on **Format**. The Format menu will appear.

2. **Click** on **AutoFormat**. The AutoFormat dialog box will open.

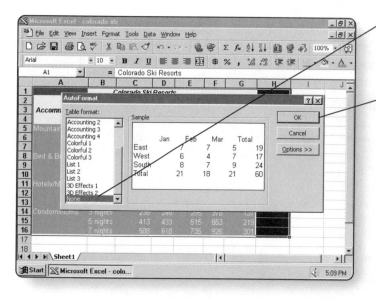

3. **Click** on **None** from the Table Format: list. The selection will be highlighted.

4. **Click** on **OK**. AutoFormat will be removed from your worksheet.

USING FONTS

Fonts are typefaces in different styles and sizes that give your text character and impact.

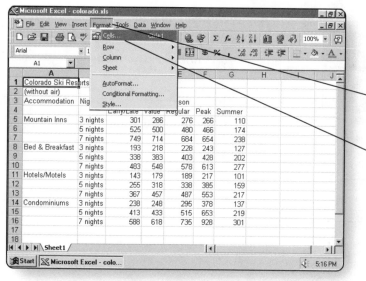

1. **Click** in the **cell(s)** containing the text you want to format. The cell(s) will be highlighted.

2. **Click** on **Format**. The Format menu will appear.

3. **Click** on **Cells**. The Format Cells dialog box will open.

4. Click on the **Font tab**. In this tab, you can select:

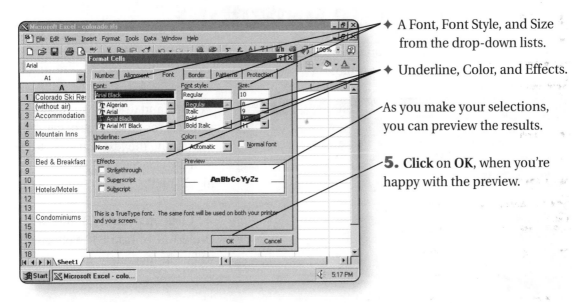

✦ A Font, Font Style, and Size from the drop-down lists.

✦ Underline, Color, and Effects.

As you make your selections, you can preview the results.

5. Click on **OK**, when you're happy with the preview.

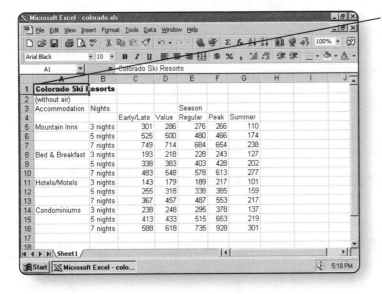

Your selections will be applied to the text.

ADDING BOLD, ITALIC, AND UNDERLINE

You can apply bold, italic, and underline formatting from the toolbar.

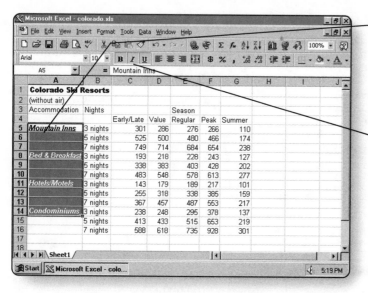

1. Click and drag the **mouse arrow** across the range of cells containing the text you want to format. The cells will be highlighted.

2. Click on the **Bold**, **Italic,** or **Underline buttons**. The effect(s) will be immediately applied to your text.

NOTE

You can select more than one attribute at a time. To remove an effect, select the text and click on the respective style button.

TIP

If the numbers become # symbols, the new font has made the text too wide to fit in the column. See Chapter 5, "Editing Worksheets," for information on adjusting column widths.

ALIGNING YOUR TEXT

You can make a worksheet easier to read by aligning the text appropriately.

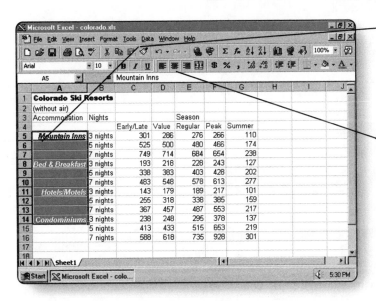

1. **Click** and **drag** the **mouse arrow** across the range of cells with the text that needs to be aligned. The cells will be highlighted.

2. **Click** on the **Left**, **Right**, or **Center align buttons**. The text will be aligned. In this example, the text has been right aligned.

Centering a Heading over More Than One Column

If you want to center a heading over more than one column, use the Merge and Center button.

1. **Click** and **drag** with the **mouse arrow** across the range of cells that need to have centered text. The cells will be highlighted.

2. **Click** on the **Merge** and **Center button**. The cells will be centered in one large cell.

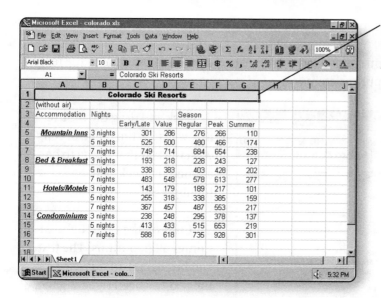

In this example, seven cells have been merged into one large cell, A1. The text has also been centered.

Other Alignment Options

You can also merge cells, wrap text in a cell, vertically align, shrink text to fit, and rotate text.

1. **Click** and **drag** the **mouse arrow** across the range that contains the text you want to format. The cells will be highlighted.

2. **Click** on **Format**. The Format menu will appear.

3. **Click** on **Cells**. The Format Cells dialog box will open.

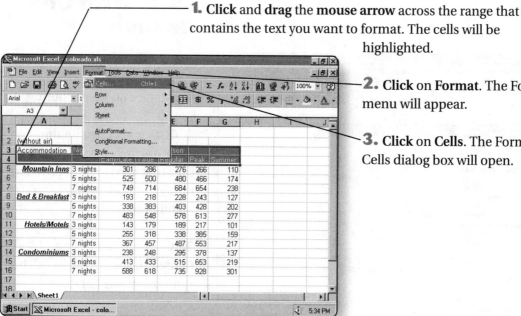

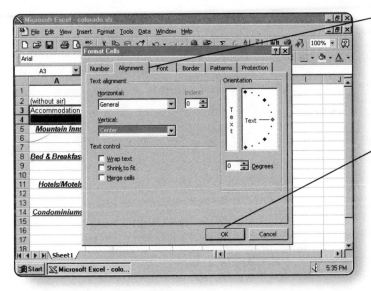

4. Click on the **Alignment tab**. The tab will come to the front.

5. Click on whatever **option** you would like to select and change.

6. Click on **OK**. The change(s) you made will be applied.

13 Formatting Numbers and Cells

The numbers you enter in a worksheet represent many values, such as dollars and cents, percentages, and dates. You need to format your raw numbers so that they're easy to recognize. You can also draw attention to particular cells with color, shading, and borders. In this chapter, you'll learn how to:

✦ Add dollar signs and decimal places

✦ Format percentages

✦ Insert today's date and select a date format

✦ Add total lines and borders

✦ Apply color backgrounds and patterns

FORMATTING CURRENCY AND PERCENTAGES

Dollar and Percentage signs enable you to quickly recognize numerical amounts in a worksheet.

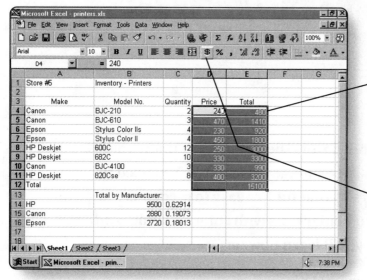

Formatting Currency

1. **Click** and **drag** with the **mouse arrow** across the range that contains or will contain currency. The cells will be highlighted.

2. **Click** on the **Currency Style button**. The selection will be formatted.

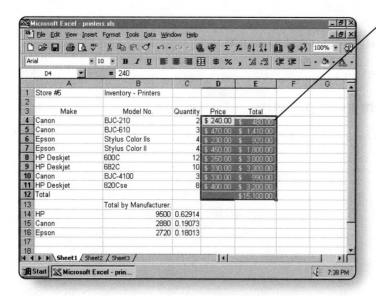

Excel will add a dollar sign, a decimal point, and cents to each entry in the selected range.

Formatting Percentages

The procedure for formatting numbers to be displayed as percentages is almost exactly the same as for currency.

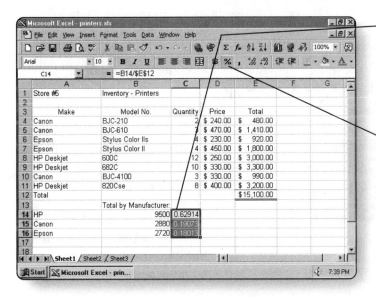

1. **Click** and **drag** with the **mouse arrow** across the range containing the data that you want to format as percentages. The cells will be highlighted.

2. **Click** on the **Percent Style button**. The selection will be formatted.

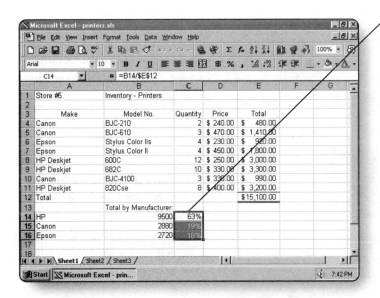

Percentages are much easier to read once they've been formatted. The numbers will be rounded and the percent sign added. Any decimal values not displayed will still be used in all calculations.

Adding and Removing Decimal Places

Amounts formatted to currency have two decimal places added for the cents. Percentages are rounded to a whole number. In either case, you may want to hide or display numbers after the decimal point.

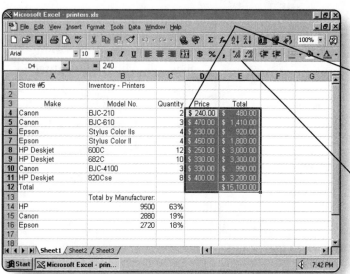

1. **Click** and **drag** with the **mouse arrow** across the range of cells that contain the numbers you want to format. The cells will be highlighted.

2. **Click twice** on either the **Increase** or **Decrease Decimal buttons**. The decimal places will increase or disappear.

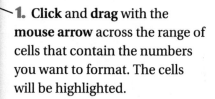

In this example, after clicking twice on the Decrease Decimal button, two decimal places have disappeared.

TIP

Be aware that if you display numbers with decimal values as whole numbers, the numbers after the decimal point will still be used in all calculations.

Formatting Dates

When you enter numbers for a date into a cell, Excel formats it as 11/16/97. You can also have the date appear in a different format.

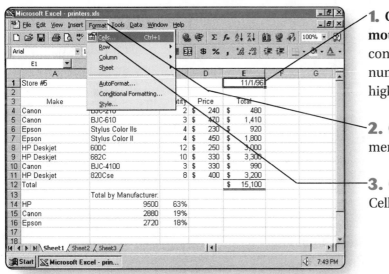

1. **Click** and **drag** with the **mouse arrow** across the range containing the date number or numbers. The cell(s) will be highlighted.

2. **Click** on **Format**. The Format menu will appear.

3. **Click** on **Cells**. The Format Cells dialog box will open.

4. **Click** on the **Number tab**. The tab will come to the front.

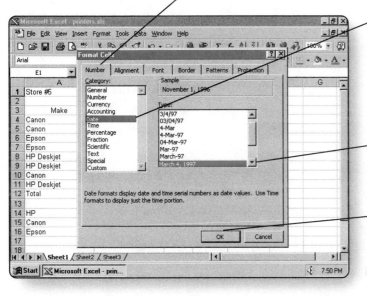

5. **Click** on **Date** in the Category: list. The item will be highlighted.

6. **Scroll** in the **Type: list** to find the format you want to use.

7. **Click** on a **format** in the Type: list. A preview will appear in the Sample area.

8. **Click** on **OK**. The Format Cells dialog box will close.

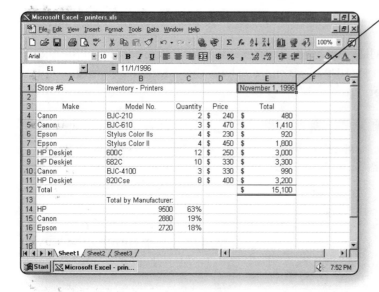

The new format for the date will appear in the cell.

INSERTING TODAY'S DATE

You can insert today's date in your worksheet so that every time you open the worksheet the date will be updated. Today's date will also always appear on your printouts, so that if you have a number of different printouts of the same worksheet you can easily see which is the most recent version.

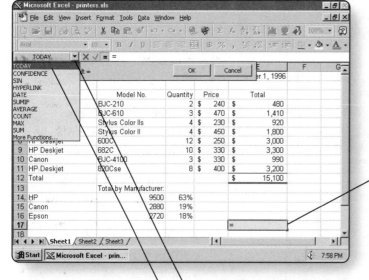

TIP

If the date isn't correct, you can correct it in the Windows Control Panel. Click on Start, Settings, Control Panel, and then the Date & Time icon.

1. **Click** on the **cell** where you want the date to appear. The cell will be highlighted.

2. **Click** on the **Edit Formula button**. The Edit Formula dialog box will open.

3. **Click** on the **down arrow** (▼) in the Formula bar. The function drop-down list will appear.

4. **Click** on **TODAY**. The TODAY box will open.

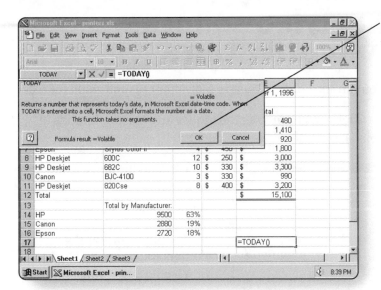

5. Click on **OK**. The TODAY box will close.

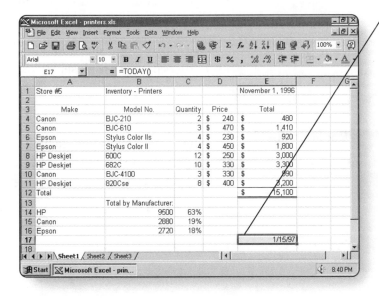

The date will appear in the selected cell.

APPLYING BORDERS AND TOTAL LINES

You can add borders (lines) to individual cells and groups of cells.

1. **Click** in a **cell** or **drag** the **mouse arrow** across a range of cells. The cell(s) will be highlighted.

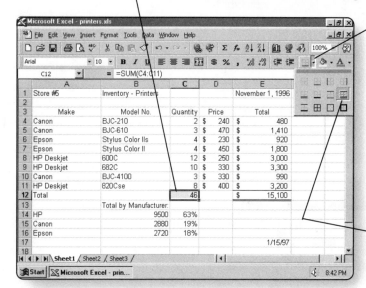

2. **Click** on the **down arrow** (▼) next to the Borders button. The Borders palette will appear.

Icons displaying how the borders will be applied to a cell or selected range (top, bottom, left, right, or a combination) and the weight of the line (thin, thick, or double) are displayed in the palette.

3. **Click** on your **selection**. The Borders palette will close.

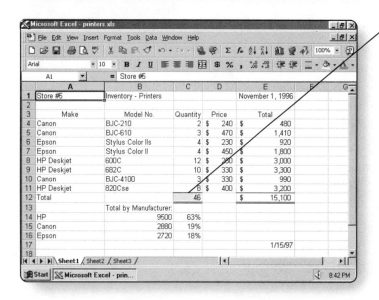

When you deselect the cell or range, you will see the border that you added.

APPLYING COLOR AND PATTERNS

If you have a color printer or you want to improve the look of your worksheet on your computer screen, you can add background colors. If you use a black and white printer, you can add shades of gray and patterns instead.

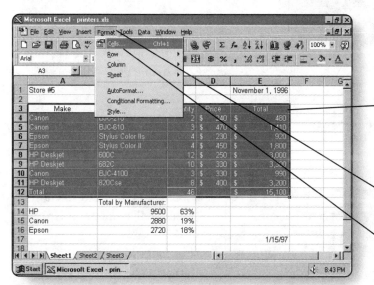

Adding a Background Color

1. Click and drag the mouse arrow across the range of cells you want to color. The cells will be highlighted.

2. Click on Format. The Format menu will appear.

3. Click on Cells. The Format Cells dialog box will open.

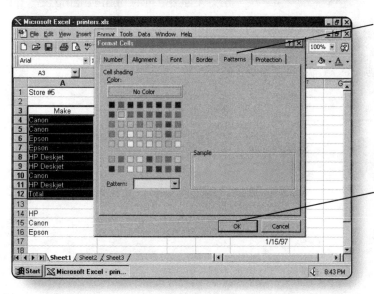

4. Click on the Patterns tab. The tab will come to the front.

5. Click on a color under the Color: heading. The color box will be highlighted and a preview will appear in the Sample box.

6. Click on OK. The color will be applied to the highlighted cells.

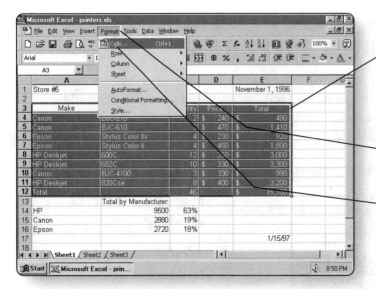

Adding a Pattern

1. **Click** and **drag** the **mouse arrow** across the range of cells you want to add a pattern to. The cells will be highlighted.

2. **Click** on **Format**. The Format menu will appear.

3. **Click** on **Cells**. The Format Cells dialog box will open.

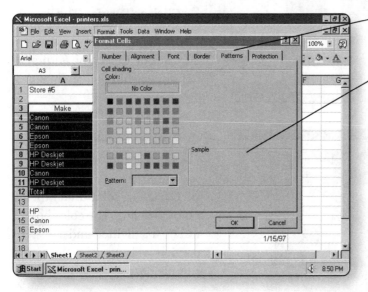

4. **Click** on the **Patterns tab**. The tab will come to the front.

There should be no color appearing in the Sample box, just the gray of the dialog box. If there is a color, click on No Color to remove it.

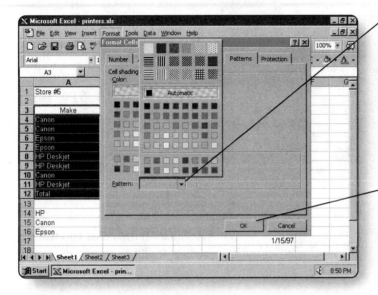

5. **Click** on the **down arrow** (▼) next to Pattern:. A palette will appear.

6. **Click** on the **pattern** you want to use.

7. **Repeat steps 5** and **6** until you find a pattern that you like.

8. **Click** on **OK**. The Format Cells dialog box will close. Your changes will appear in the worksheet.

TIP

Remember that the pattern is a background and if you will be entering data into the cells in the selected range, you need to select a light pattern, so that the data can still be read.

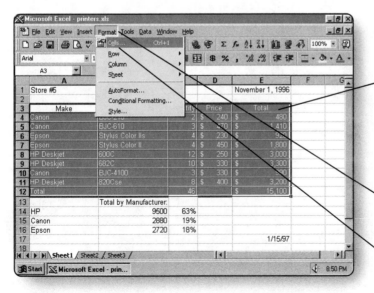

Adding a Colored Pattern

1. **Click** and **drag** the **mouse arrow** across the range of cells you want to add a colored pattern to. The cells will be highlighted.

2. **Click** on **Format**. The Format menu will appear.

3. **Click** on **Cells**. The Format Cells dialog box will open.

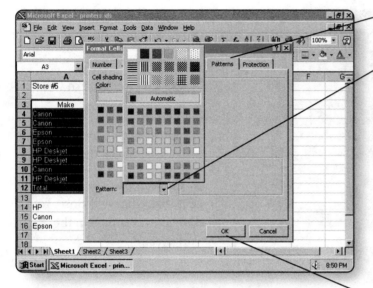

4. **Click** on the **Patterns tab**. The tab will come to the front.

5. **Click** on the **down arrow** (▼) next to Pattern:. A palette will appear.

6. **Click** on the **pattern** you want to use. The palette will close and the pattern will appear in the Sample box.

7. **Click** on the **color** you want to use. It will appear in the Sample box with the pattern.

8. **Click** on **OK**. The Format Cells dialog box will close. Your changes will appear in the selected cells.

14 Adding Clip Art and WordArt to a Worksheet

Whether you need to make a presentation of financial information to the Board of Directors or PTA, you can add interest and flair to your document with pictures and WordArt. In this chapter, you'll learn how to:

✦ Add clip art and adjust its size and placement

✦ Remove the border from clip art and make the background transparent

✦ Adjust the contrast and brightness of clip art

✦ Add and edit WordArt

ADDING CLIP ART

Clip art is a graphic or drawing file that has been created for you to use. By using clip art, you can quickly and easily add illustrations to your document.

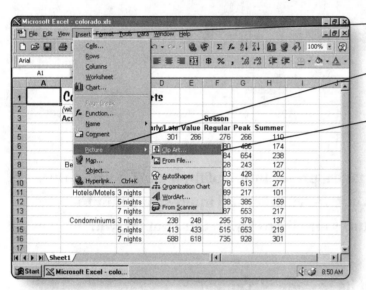

1. **Click** on **Insert**. The Insert menu will appear.

2. **Click** on **Picture**. A submenu will appear.

3. **Click** on **Clip Art**. The Microsoft Clip Gallery 3.0 dialog box will open.

TIP

If you don't currently have the Office 97 CD in your CD-ROM drive, a dialog box will open telling you that Additional Clips are Available on CD. Click on OK to continue. You will have considerably more clip art to choose from if you use the Office 97 CD. It's certainly worth taking the time to locate and insert your CD.

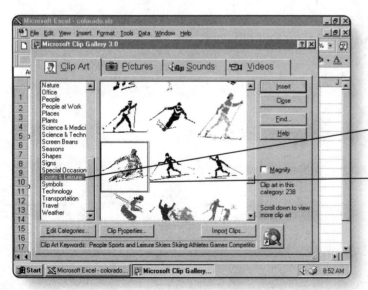

4. **Click** on a **category**. The category will be highlighted.

5. **Click** on a **clip art image**. A border will appear around your selection.

6. **Click** on **Insert**. The clip art will be placed on top of your worksheet.

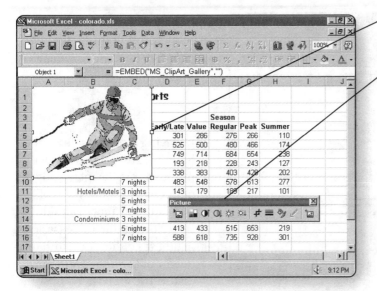

Selection handles will be visible around the box.

The picture toolbar will also open.

ADJUSTING THE SIZE AND LOCATION OF CLIP ART

Whenever you use clip art, you will need to adjust its size and location so that it fits appropriately with your data. The graphic needs to be big enough to be interesting but not so large that it detracts from the data.

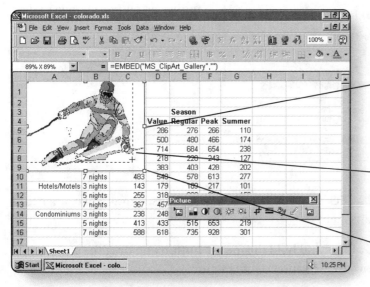

Adjusting the Size of Clip Art

1. **Move** the **mouse arrow** over one of the selection handles. The arrow will change to a double-headed arrow.

2. **Press** and **hold** the **mouse button** until the pointer changes to a crosshair.

3. **Drag** the **selection handle** in or out.

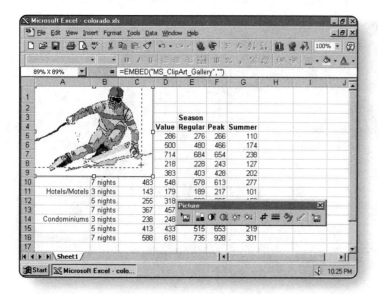

4. **Release** the **mouse button**. The picture will shrink or expand, depending on which way you drag.

NOTE

Dragging a corner selection handle sizes a clip art image proportionately; increasing or decreasing both the width and height. Dragging a side selection handle increases or decreases either the width or height of the image and may distort the graphic.

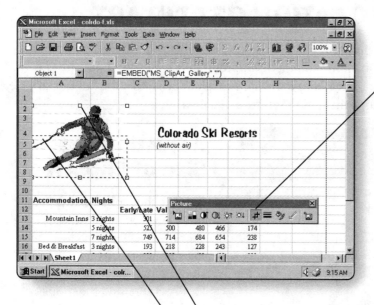

Cropping the Clip Art Image

1. **Click** on the **Crop button** on the Picture toolbar. The mouse arrow will change to the cropping tool.

2. **Click** on a **selection box**. The mouse arrow will change to a crosshair.

3. **Press** and **hold** the **mouse button** and **drag** the **crosshair** in toward the center of the picture.

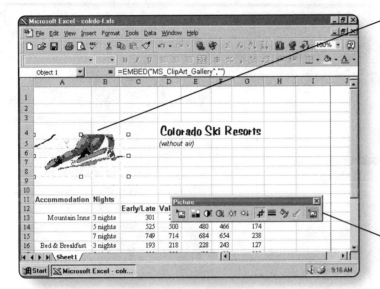

4. Release the **mouse button**. The clip art will be adjusted to the new size.

NOTE

To deselect the cropping tool, click anywhere outside of the graphic image.

TIP

If you crop too much, simply click on the Reset Picture button on the Picture toolbar and the cropping will be removed. This button will also return color, brightness, and contrast changes to their original settings.

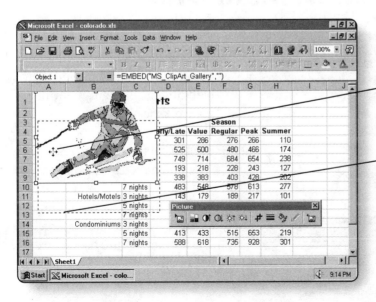

Moving the Clip Art Image

1. Move the **mouse arrow** over the picture. It will change to a four-headed arrow.

2. Press and **hold** the **mouse button** and **drag** the **picture** to a new location.

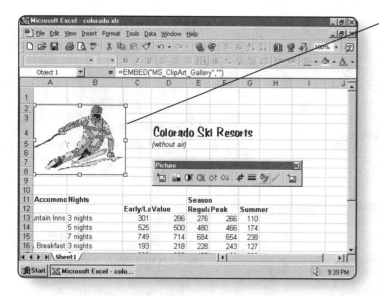

3. **Release** the **mouse button**. The clip art will be moved.

NOTE

When you finally decide where the clip art image looks best, you may find you need to move your data so that it isn't obscured by the graphic. This is easy. You can use the cut and paste commands covered in Chapter 5, "Editing Worksheets," or you can insert some blank columns or rows (see Chapter 4).

REMOVING THE IMAGE BOX AND BLENDING THE BACKGROUND

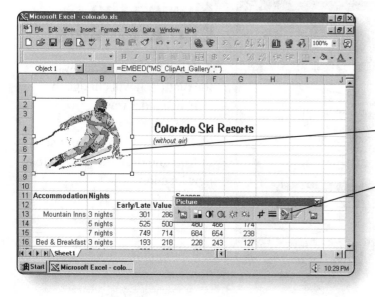

You can improve the look of your document by removing the box around the picture and then blending the background with the worksheet.

1. **Click** on the **picture**. The selection handles will appear.

2. **Click** on the **Format Picture button** on the Picture toolbar. The Format Picture dialog box will open.

3. **Click** on the **Colors and Lines tab**. The tab will come to the front.

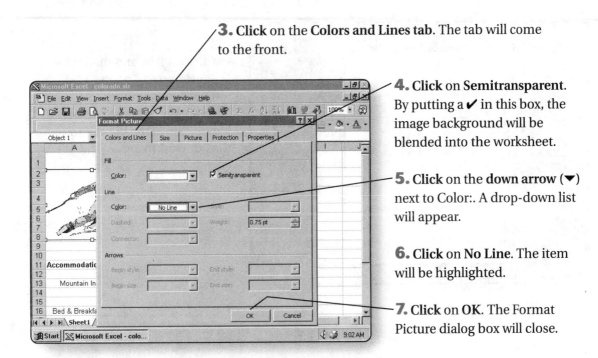

4. **Click** on **Semitransparent**. By putting a ✔ in this box, the image background will be blended into the worksheet.

5. **Click** on the **down arrow (▼)** next to Color:. A drop-down list will appear.

6. **Click** on **No Line**. The item will be highlighted.

7. **Click** on **OK**. The Format Picture dialog box will close.

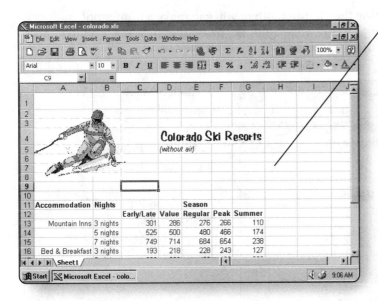

8. **Click** on the **worksheet** outside of the graphic. The picture will be deselected and blend into the worksheet.

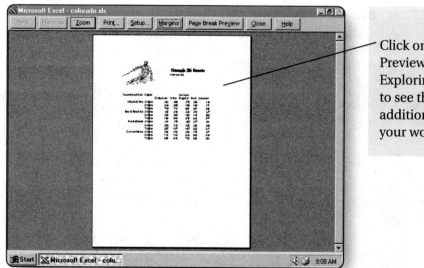

TIP

Click on File, and then Print Preview (see Chapter 11, Exploring Printing Options) to see the full effect of the addition of the picture to your worksheet.

ADJUSTING THE QUALITY OF THE PICTURE

Using the Picture toolbar, you can make a number of adjustments to the picture after you've inserted it. The toolbar may not be visible.

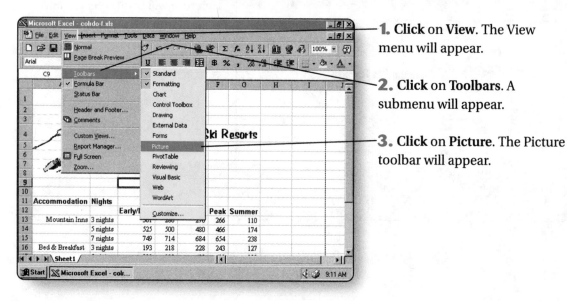

1. **Click** on **View**. The View menu will appear.

2. **Click** on **Toolbars**. A submenu will appear.

3. **Click** on **Picture**. The Picture toolbar will appear.

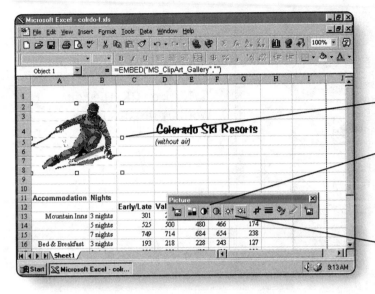

Adjusting the Contrast and Brightness

1. **Click** on a **picture**. The selection handles will appear.

2. **Click** on the **More Contrast** or **Less Contrast button**. The contrast in the picture will increase or decrease.

3. **Click** on the **More Brightness** or **Less Brightness button**. The brightness in the picture will increase or decrease.

ADDING WORDART

Fonts can add some interest to your text but for more dramatic effects try using WordArt. You can apply amazing color schemes, 3-D effects, and sculpt your words into various shapes.

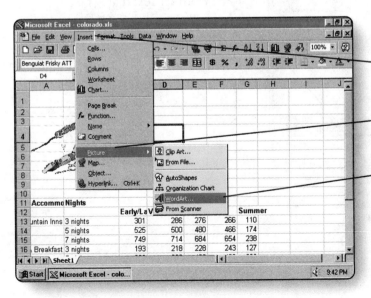

1. **Click** on **Insert**. The Insert menu will appear.

2. **Click** on **Picture**. A submenu will appear.

3. **Click** on **WordArt**. The WordArt Gallery dialog box will open.

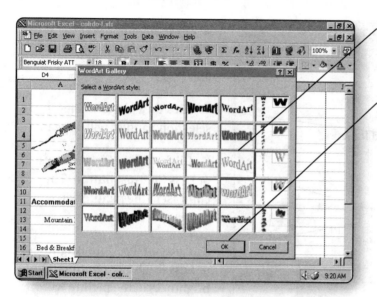

4. Click on a **style** in the WordArt Gallery. A border will appear around your selection.

5. Click on **OK**. The Edit WordArt Text dialog box will open.

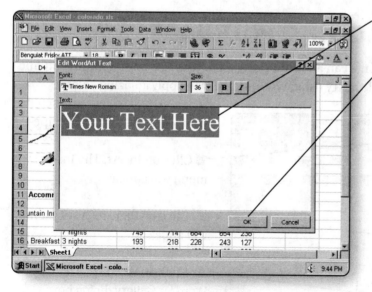

6. Type in **text** to replace "Type Text Here."

7. Click on **OK**. The Edit WordArt Text dialog box will close.

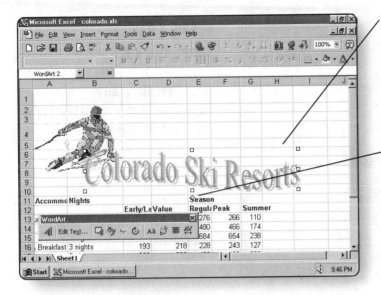

The text will appear in a layer above your worksheet surrounded by selection handles.

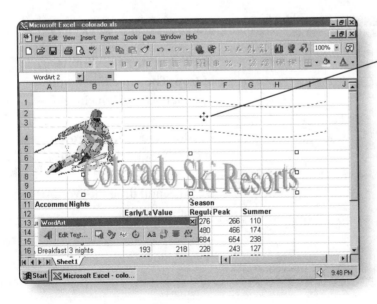

Moving WordArt

1. **Move** the **mouse arrow** over the WordArt. The mouse arrow will change to a four-headed arrow.

2. **Press** and **hold** the **mouse button** and **drag** the **WordArt** to a new location.

3. **Release** the **mouse button**. The WordArt will be moved.

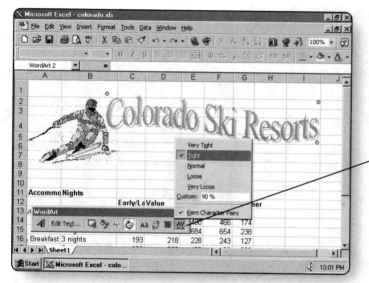

EDITING WORDART

You can make many adjustments to WordArt from the WordArt toolbar.

1. Click on the **WordArt Character Spacing button** on the WordArt toolbar. The spacing between the letters will be adjusted.

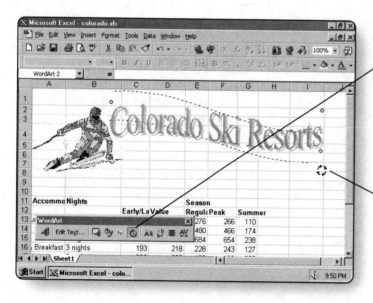

Rotating WordArt

1. Click on the **Free Rotate button**. The selection handles will change to green circles.

2. Move the **mouse arrow** over one of the selection handles.

3. Click and **drag** the WordArt to a new angle.

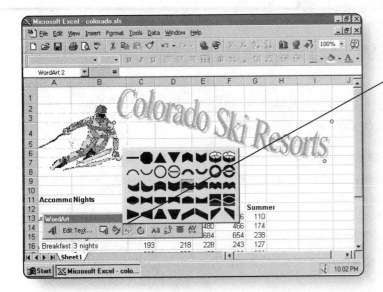

Changing the WordArt Shape

1. **Click** on the **WordArt Shape button**. A palette will appear.

2. **Click** on a **different shape** for the letters to follow.

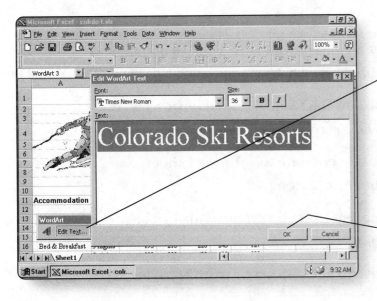

Editing WordArt Text

1. **Click** on the **Edit Text button** to correct typing errors or make changes to the text. The Edit WordArt Text dialog box will open.

2. **Make** your **changes**.

3. **Click** on **OK**. Your changes will appear in the document.

PART III REVIEW QUESTIONS

1. Why would you want to use the Excel AutoFormat feature? *See "Using AutoFormat" in Chapter 12.*

2. Why does Excel sometimes replace your entries with # signs when you change the font or font size? *See "Using Fonts" in Chapter 12.*

3. How can you center a head over more than one column? *See "Centering a Heading over More Than One Column" in Chapter 12.*

4. Why do you need to format numbers? *See the introduction in Chapter 13.*

5. How can you quickly format numbers in a cell as dollars and cents? *See "Formatting Currency" in Chapter 13.*

6. What do the Increase and Decrease Decimal buttons do in Excel? *See "Adding and Removing Decimal Places" in Chapter 13.*

7. How can you add the current date to your worksheet? *See "Inserting Today's Date" in Chapter 13.*

8. What is the difference between clip art and WordArt? *See the introduction in Chapter 14.*

9. What menu do you use to add clip art or WordArt to an Excel worksheet? *See the introduction in Chapter 14.*

10. How can you move or resize clip art or WordArt after you've added it to a worksheet? *See the introduction in Chapter 14.*

PART IV

Creating Charts and Maps of Your Data

15 Generating a Chart

If you've ever spent hours creating charts on graph paper, you'll really appreciate how easy creating a chart is in Excel. Just make a few choices and you will see your data transformed into a 3-D pie chart complete with data labels. In this chapter, you'll learn how to:

✦ **Use the Chart Wizard to create a chart**

✦ **Select colors and fonts for chart titles and labels**

✦ **Angle text labels**

CREATING A CHART WITH THE CHART WIZARD

The Chart Wizard is really amazing. It enables you to create a sophisticated chart of your data in just a few minutes.

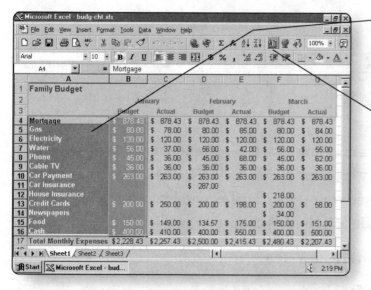

1. Click and drag with the mouse arrow across the range that you want to chart. The cells will be highlighted.

2. Click on the Chart Wizard button. The Chart Wizard – Step 1 of 4 dialog box will open.

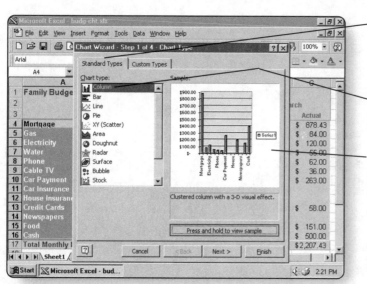

3. Click on the Standard Types tab. The tab will come to the front.

4. Click on a chart type. The item will be highlighted.

In the Sample: area, you'll see an example of what that particular chart will look like and a written description.

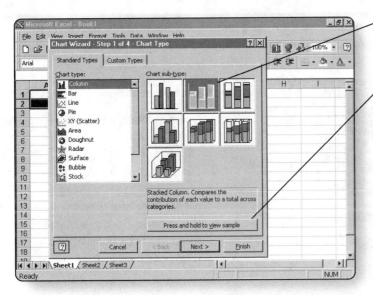

5. Click on an **option** in the Chart sub-type: area. The item will be highlighted.

6. Click on the **Press and hold to view sample button**. You will be able to see what your data will look like if you choose a particular chart type. This can be helpful if you're not very experienced creating charts. For example, if your data varies from very low numbers to very high numbers, a column chart may not show anything very useful.

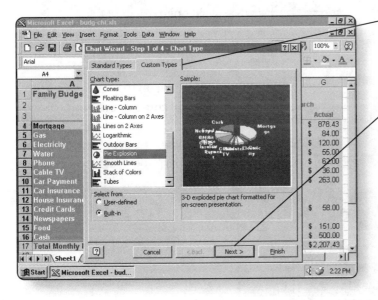

7. Click on the **Custom Types** tab. You will be able to view charts that have the background, colors, and fonts preselected.

8. Click on **Next**, when the chart type you want to use is displayed. The Chart Wizard – Step 2 of 4 dialog box will open.

If you selected your data before clicking on the Chart Wizard in step 2, the data will appear in the Data Range tab.

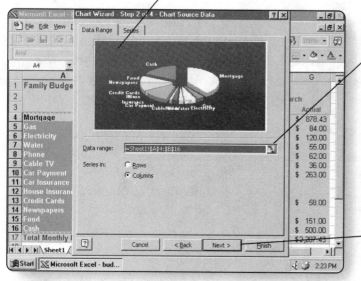

9. **Click** on **Next**. The Chart Wizard – Step 3 of 4 dialog box will open.

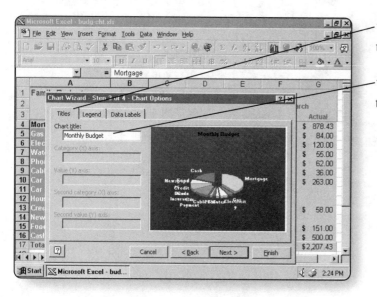

10. **Click** on the **Titles tab**. The tab will come to the front.

11. **Type** a **title** for your chart in the Chart title: text box.

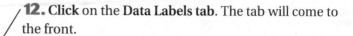

12. **Click** on the **Data Labels tab**. The tab will come to the front.

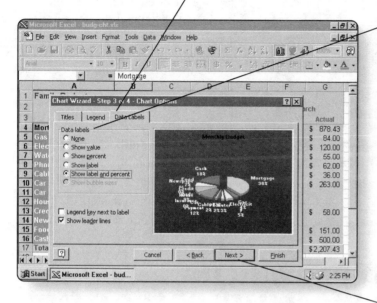

13a. **Click** on **one** of the **Data labels options**. For example, you can choose to display the actual numerical value the chart element represents next to the element by selecting Show Values. You can also label the various data series (1, 2, 3, and so on) by selecting Show Labels.

OR

13b. **Click** on **None** in the Data labels box, if you would like no options to be applied.

14. **Click** on **Next**. The Chart Wizard – Step 4 of 4 dialog box will open.

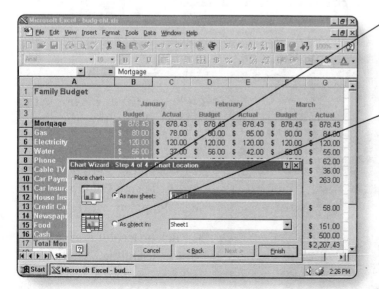

15a. **Click** on **As new sheet:** to create your chart in a new worksheet.

OR

15b. **Click** on **As object in:** to add it to the worksheet that contains the data, so that you can print both the data and the chart on the same page.

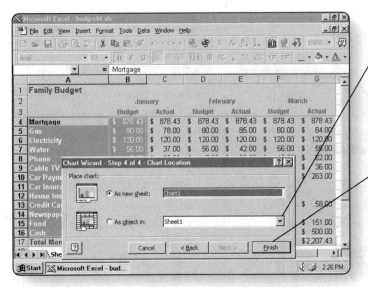

NOTE

If you select As object in:, you also need to click on the down arrow (▼) to select what worksheet the object should appear in.

16. **Click** on **Finish**. The chart will appear either in the current worksheet or in a new worksheet called "Chart1," depending on your selection in step 15. The Chart toolbar will also open.

IMPROVING THE READABILITY OF THE CHART

Although the Wizard formats the chart, you may need to make some changes to improve its readability.

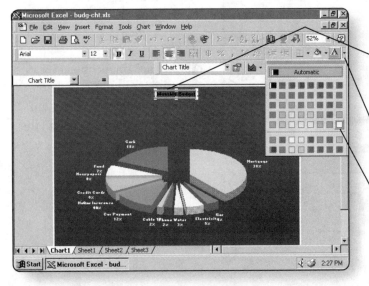

Formatting Titles and Labels

1. **Click** on the **title**. A box with eight handles will appear around it.

2. **Click** on the **down arrow** (▼) next to the Font Color button. The color palette will open.

3. **Click** on a **color** that will be more visible against the background color in your chart. The new color will appear on the title.

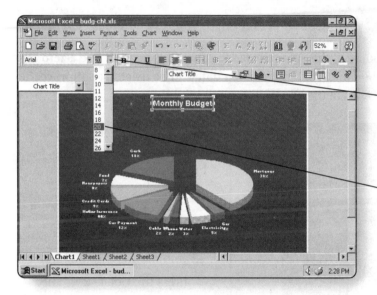

If the text is now easier to read but still a little small, you can change the font size.

4. Click on the **Font Size button**, while the title is still selected. A drop-down list will appear.

5. Click on a **larger size**. The title will appear in the new size.

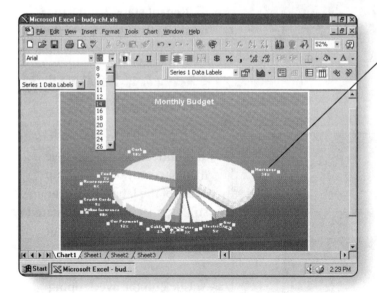

TIP

To change the font or font size for the labels, click on any label and all of them will be selected. Follow steps 2 through 5 to format the labels.

Deleting Labels from Your Chart

Some of the data selected for this chart actually had a zero for the month of January. That data can be deleted to improve the clarity of the labels.

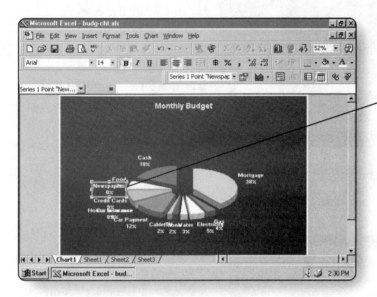

1. **Click** on a **label** to select them all. The labels will be highlighted.

2. **Click** on the **label** you want to delete. A box with eight handles will appear around it.

3. **Press** the **Delete key**. The label will be deleted.

4. **Repeat steps 2** and **3** to remove all unnecessary labels.

Placing Labels at an Angle

With the labels in a larger font and unnecessary labels deleted, the chart may be clearer but some of the labels may overlap still. Overlap can be eliminated by simply placing the text at an angle.

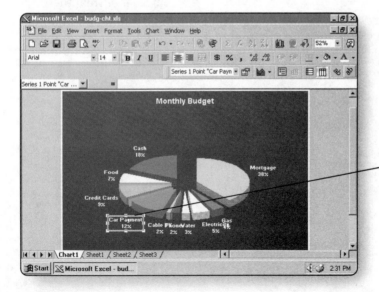

1. **Click** on the **overlapping label**. A box with eight handles will appear around it.

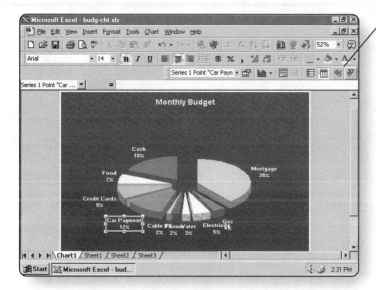

2. **Click** on either the **Angle Text Upward** or the **Angle Text Downward button**. The two labels will no longer overlap one another.

Moving Labels

If your text labels are still too close to one another or not lined up accurately, you can move them.

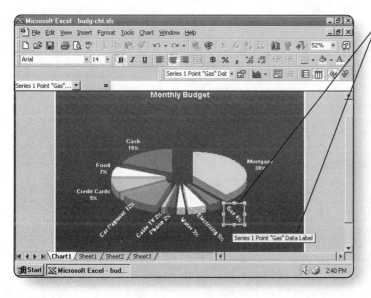

1. **Click** on the **label** you want to move. A box with eight handles will appear. Also an explanation of the label and what series it represents will appear to assist you in choosing the correct label.

2. **Click** on the **border** of the label box and **drag** it to a new location. The box will be moved.

TIP

If you drag the label too far, Excel will think that the label is not close enough to the correct slice of pie so it will add a connecting line. How helpful!

16 Adding Special Effects to Your Chart

Excel has built-in special effects that can really give your charts pizzazz! In this chapter, you'll learn how to:

✦ Create a 3-D bar chart

✦ Add series labels

✦ Add a legend

✦ Use gradients, textures, and preset color backgrounds

CREATING A 3-D BAR CHART

The purpose of this chart is to compare the budget amounts with actual expenses for January and to demonstrate some of the many built-in special effects that are available in Excel.

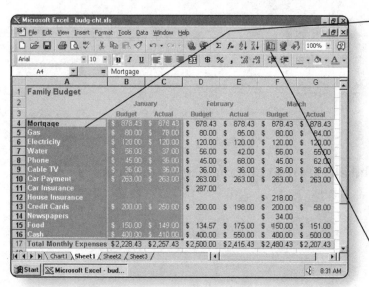

1. Click and drag across **two columns** of data, including the row labels. The cells will be highlighted.

NOTE

Do not include the column labels or the column totals because you won't create a useful chart.

2. Click on the **Chart Wizard button**. The Chart Wizard – Step 1 of 4 dialog box will open.

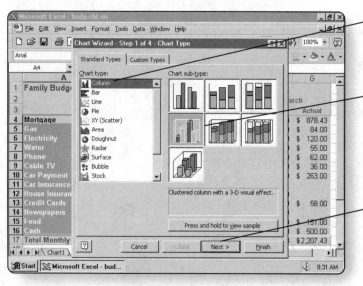

3. Click on **Column** in the Chart type: list. The item will be highlighted.

4. Click on the **Clustered column with a 3-D visual effect chart** (2nd row, far left) in the Chart sub-type: box. The chart will be highlighted.

5. Click on **Next**. The Chart Wizard – Step 2 of 4 dialog box will open.

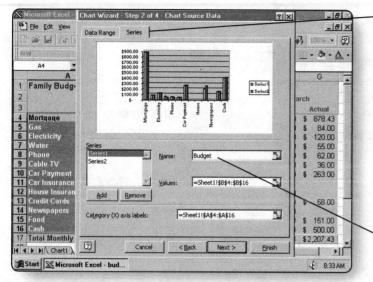

6. Click on the **Series tab**. The tab will come to the front.

You can label a series with a name or a value. *Series* refers to a collection of related data whether it's in columns or rows. In this example, the Budget data in the worksheet is one series, and the Actual data is another series.

7. Type a **name** for the Series1 data in the Name: text box. In this example, the name "Budget" is used.

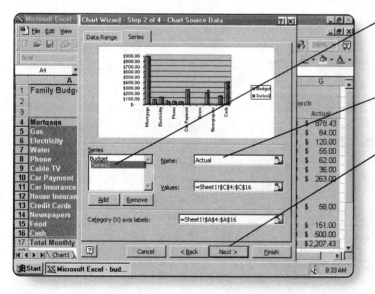

8. Click on **Series2** in the Series: text box. The item will be highlighted.

9. Type **Actual** in the Name: text box.

10. Click on **Next**. The Chart Wizard – Step 3 of 4 dialog box will open.

11. Click on the **Titles tab**. The tab will come to the front.

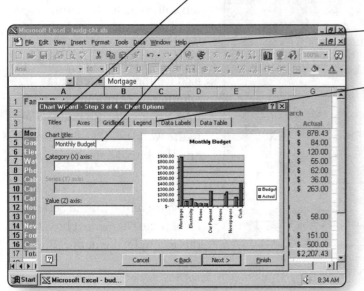

12. Type Monthly Budget in the Chart title: text box.

13. Click on the **Legend tab**. The tab will come to the front.

NOTE

A *legend* is the same in a chart as it is on any map. It's an explanation of symbols. In this case, it shows which color represents each series of data.

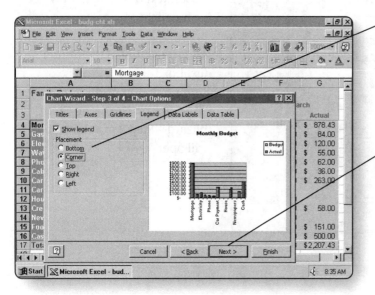

14. Click on an **option** in the Placement box to place the Legend at the Top, Bottom, Left, Right, or Corner of the chart area. The option will be highlighted.

15. Click on **Next**. The Chart Wizard – Step 4 of 4 dialog box will open.

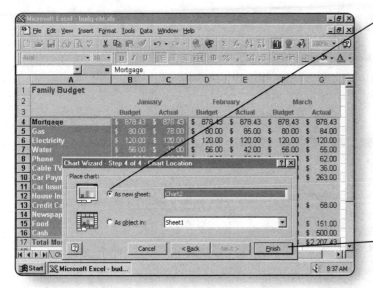

16. **Click** on **As new sheet:** to create the chart as a new worksheet. The option will be highlighted.

TIP

Selecting to make a chart an object in the current worksheet is covered in Chapter 15, "Generating a Chart."

17. **Click** on **Finish**. The dialog box will close.

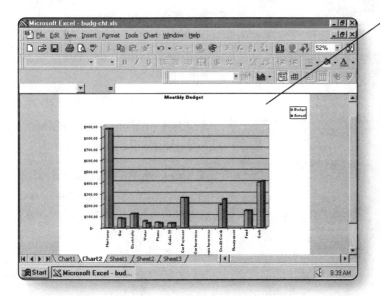

Your new chart will appear as a new worksheet and the Chart toolbar will open.

NOTE

At any time, before you click on Finish, you can click on the Back button to return to previous screens and make changes to your selections.

ADDING SPECIAL EFFECTS

The chart created has a 3-D effect. You can add more special effects including gradients, textures, and specially designed color combinations.

Adding a Gradient

You can add a color background with a gradient to liven up your chart.

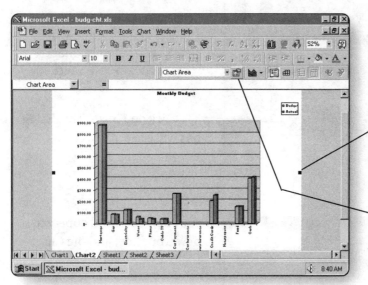

1. **Click** on the **outside** of the **chart** on the background chart area. Handles will appear at the edge of the chart.

2. **Click** on the **Format Chart button** on the Chart toolbar. The Format Chart Area dialog box will open.

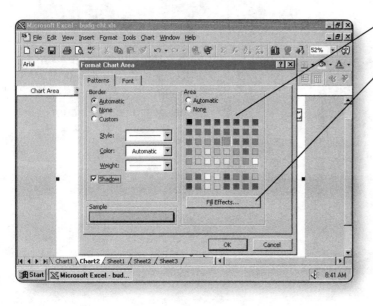

3. **Click** on a chart **Area color**. The color will be highlighted.

4. **Click** on **Fill Effects** to modify the appearance of the chart area color. The Fill Effects dialog box will open.

TIP

You can also add a Shadow effect or border around the chart area in the Border area of the dialog box. For the border, you can select different line styles, colors, or weights.

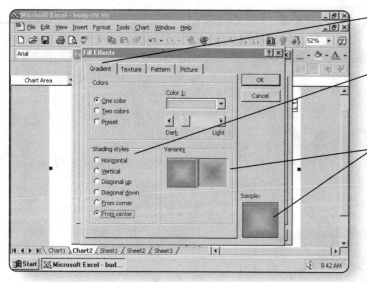

5. **Click** on the **Gradient tab**. The tab will come to the front.

6. **Click** on **one** of the **styles** in the Shading styles box. The item will be highlighted.

7. **Click** on **one** of the **Variants**. You will see the effect you've selected in the Sample: box.

8. **Click** on **OK**. The Fill Effects dialog box will close and the Format Chart Area dialog box will appear.

9. **Click** on **OK**. The Format Chart Area dialog box will close.

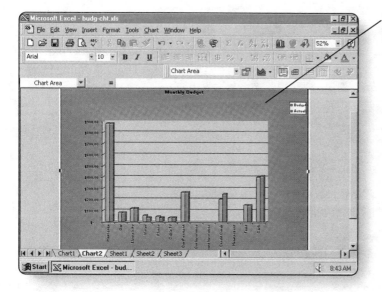

You'll now be able to view the effects you added to your chart.

Adding a Texture

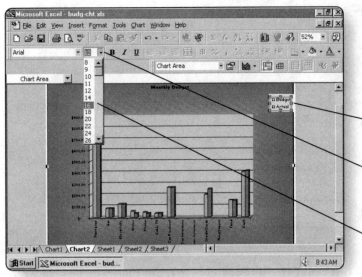

You can also add a special effect to the background of the legend. Before you add any special effects to the legend, you should enlarge it.

1. **Click** on the **legend**. Handles will appear.

2. **Click** on the **Font Size button.** A drop-down list will appear.

3. **Click** on a **larger size**. The font size of the legend will increase.

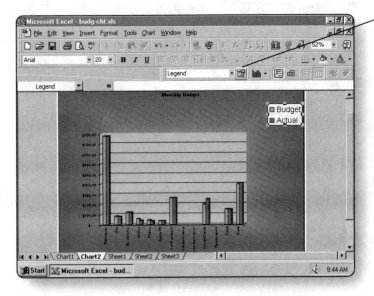

4. **Click** on the **Chart Format button** on the Chart toolbar. The Format Legend dialog box will open.

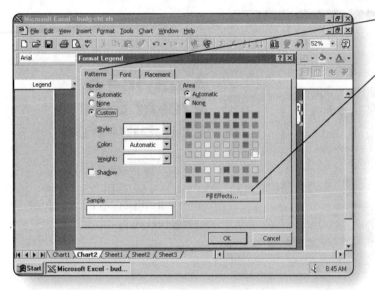

5. **Click** on the **Patterns tab**. The tab will come to the front.

6. **Click** on **Fill Effects**. The Fill Effects dialog box will open.

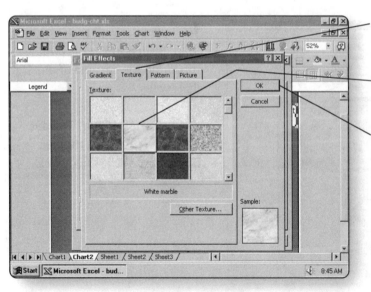

7. **Click** on the **Texture tab**. The tab will come to the front.

8. **Click** on a **texture**. The item will be highlighted.

9. **Click** on **OK**. The Fill Effects dialog box will close and the Format Legend dialog box will appear.

10. **Click** on **OK**. The Format Legend dialog box will close.

TIP

Remember that the text for the Legend must be legible so it's a good idea to select a faint, simple texture pattern so that it doesn't obscure the legend text.

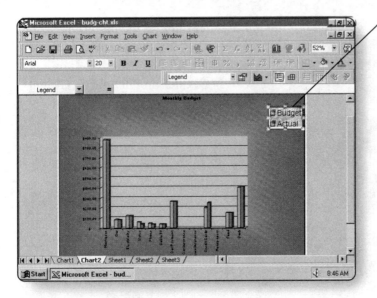

The texture effects will be added to the legend.

Applying a Preset Color Combination

To add real pizzazz to your chart, you can apply a preset color combination to the chart or legend background.

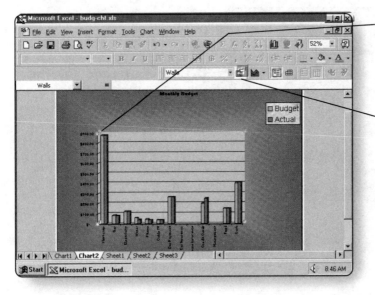

1. Click in the **wall area** of your chart. Selection handles will appear on the corners of the chart walls.

2. Click on the **Chart Format button** on the Chart toolbar. The Format Walls dialog box will open.

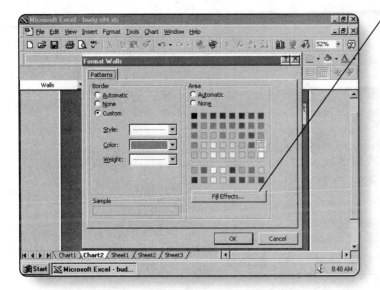

3. **Click** on **Fill Effects**. The Fill Effects dialog box will open.

4. **Click** on the **Gradient tab**. The tab will come to the front.

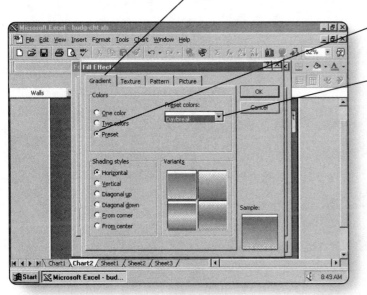

5. **Click** on **Preset** in the Colors box. The item will be selected.

6. **Click** on the **down arrow** (▼) next to Preset colors:. A drop-down list will appear.

7. **Click** on **one** of the **preset color combinations** available. You will be able to view your selection in the Sample: area.

8. **Click** on **OK**. The Fill Effects dialog box will close and the Format Walls dialog box will appear.

9. **Click** on **OK**. The Format Walls dialog box will close and the new effects will be added to your chart.

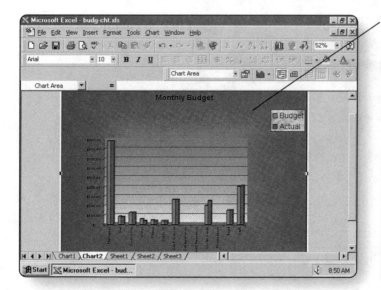

This chart suffers from the addition of too much color and too many special effects, but it does give you an idea of the range of stunning effects available within Excel.

TIP

To make the chart title larger, click on it once. The selection handles will appear. Click on a larger font from the font size drop-down list.

17 Creating a Map

Business data is often related to geographic areas. Excel has a great feature which enables you to plot data directly on a map. In this chapter, you'll learn how to:

✦ Create a map

✦ Add labels and text to the map

✦ Add features such as cities, airports, or highways

✦ Place the map in your worksheet

MAKING A MAP

In this example, the worksheet contains Australian sales data by state. You can create a map to display this data.

1. Click and **drag** the **mouse arrow** across the columns with the state names and sales data. The cells will be highlighted.

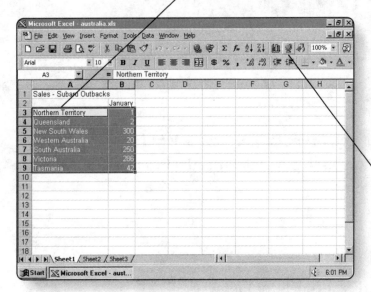

NOTE

It is important to include labels which Excel will recognize as geographic data or it won't be able to create a map.

2. Click on the **Map button**. The mouse arrow will change to a crosshair when you move it back over the worksheet area.

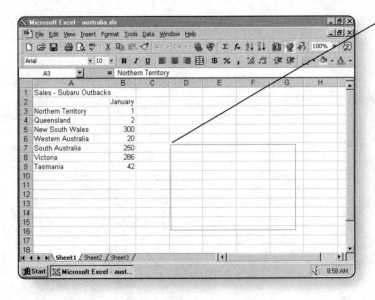

3. Click on the **cell** that will be the top left corner of your map and then **drag** the **crosshair** down and to the right to create a box for the map. Based on the information you selected, Excel will insert a map of Australia and place the map, with the states shaded in proportion to the sales data, inside the box.

TIP

If the states had been New York, Connecticut, and Rhode Island, Excel would have drawn a map of North America. To focus on the right area of North America, you would click the Center Map button on the Map toolbar, and then click on the Northeast area of the map. To further enlarge the area, you would click on the Zoom Percentage of Map down arrow (▼) and select from options up to 1000% in the drop-down list.

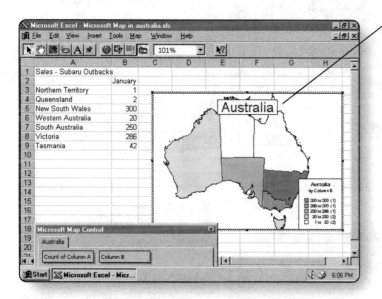

Excel will even add a title and legend for your map. Also the Map toolbar will replace the standard toolbars and the Microsoft Map Control dialog box will open.

ADDING LABELS AND TEXT

The effectiveness of the map can be improved by adding text beyond the legend. You can either add labels from the worksheet or you can add your own text.

Adding Labels

1. **Click** on the **Map Labels button** on the Map toolbar. The Map Labels dialog box will open.

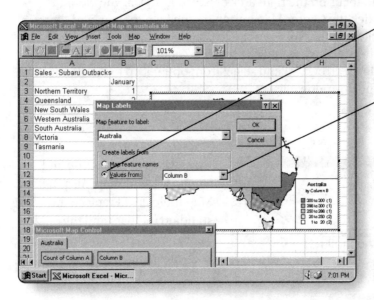

2. **Click** on **Values From:** in the Create labels from box. The item will be highlighted.

3. **Click** on the **down arrow** (▼) next to Values From:. A drop-down list will appear.

4. **Click** on **Column B**. The sales numbers will be added to the map.

5. **Click** on **OK**. The Map Labels dialog box will close.

6. **Move** the **mouse arrow** across the map. Notice that the correct sales number will appear as you move the mouse arrow across the corresponding state.

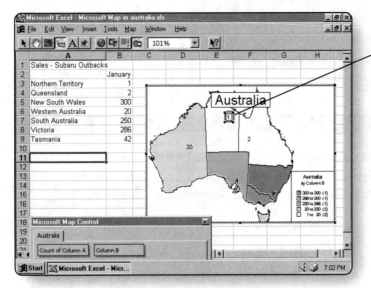

7. **Click** in the **appropriate state** to place the sales number on the map. Selection handles will appear around the number.

8. **Click anywhere** on the map. The selection handles will be removed and the number will remain.

9. **Repeat steps 6** through **8** to add the remaining sales numbers.

Adding Text

You can add text to the map. In this example, the names of the salesmen will be added.

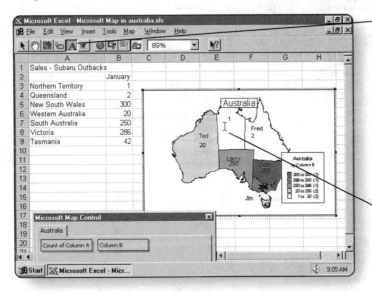

1. Click on the **Add Text button** on the Map toolbar. The mouse arrow will change to an I-beam when you move it back over the worksheet area.

2. Move the **mouse arrow** across the map to where you want to add text.

3. Click on the **map** where you want to place a name. An insertion point will appear.

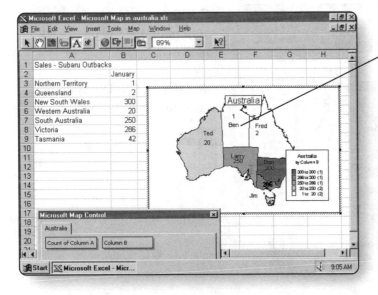

4. Type a **name**.

5. Press the **Enter key**. The name will remain on the map.

ADDING CITIES, HIGHWAYS, AND AIRPORTS

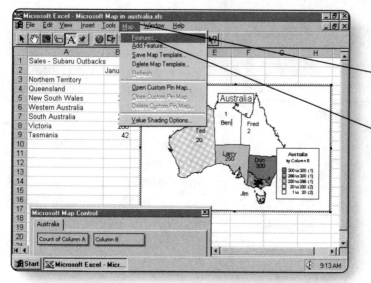

Excel has more built-in features that you can add to your map.

1. Click on **Map**. The Map menu will appear.

2. Click on **Features**. The Map Features dialog box will open.

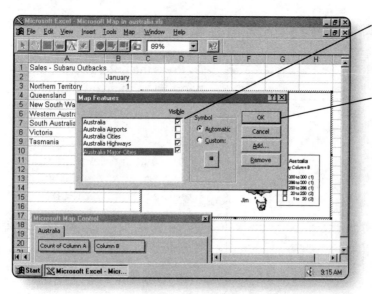

3. Click on a **feature** to use it in your map. A ✔ will be placed next to it.

4. Click on **OK**. The Map Features dialog box will close.

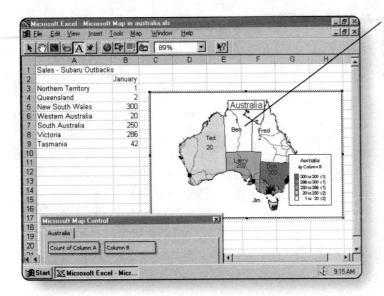

Now you can see why Ben only sold one vehicle. There aren't a lot of roads in the Northern Territory!

EDITING TEXT

You will probably need to edit both the title and legend created by Excel.

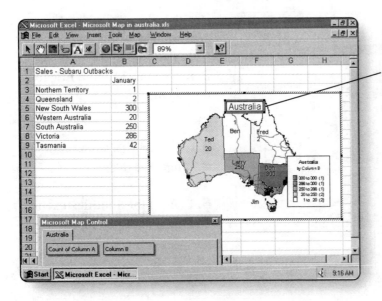

Editing the Title

1. Click on the **title** in the map. Selection handles and a border will appear around the title.

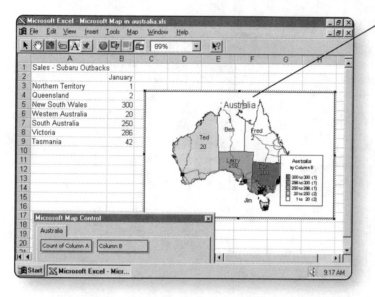

2. **Click** on the **title again** to place the insertion point. The border and handles will disappear.

You can now edit the text in the normal way. Move around with the arrow keys and type to insert text. Press the delete or backspace keys, if you make a mistake, and the Enter key when you are finished.

Editing the Legend

1. **Click twice** on the **legend**. The Format Properties dialog box will open.

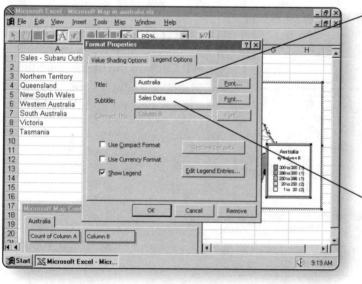

2. **Click** in the **Title: text box**. The text will be highlighted.

3a. **Type** to **add a new title** to the legend.

OR

3b. **Press** the **Delete key** to eliminate the title.

4. **Click** in the **Subtitle: text box**. The text will be highlighted.

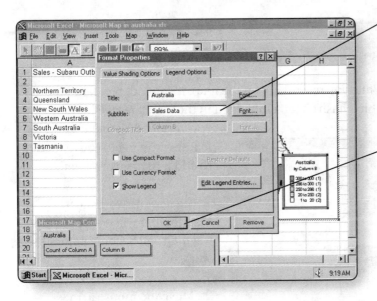

5a. Type to **add a new subtitle** to the legend.

OR

5b. Press the **Delete key** to eliminate the subtitle.

6. Click on **OK**. The Format Properties dialog box will close.

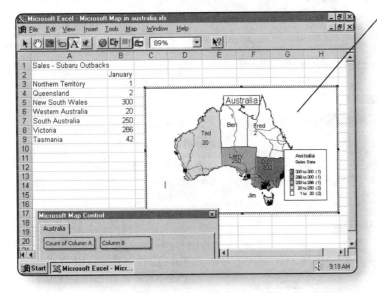

The changes you made to the legend will appear in the map.

TIP

To delete the legend, click in the Show Legend check box in the Format Properties dialog box to remove the ✔.

INSERTING THE MAP IN THE WORKSHEET

While you're working on the map, it's an independent object which hasn't been embedded in the worksheet yet. When you've added all the text and features you need, you're ready to add it to the worksheet.

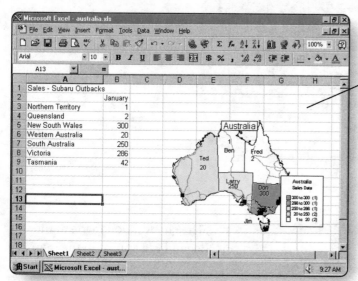

1. **Click** in the **worksheet**. The Map toolbar will disappear and the map will become part of the worksheet.

2. **Move** the **mouse arrow** across the map. The mouse arrow will change to a four-headed arrow.

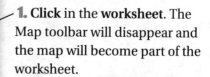

3. **Click** on the **map** and **drag** it to where you want it to appear within your worksheet.

TIP

To edit the map once it's embedded in the worksheet, click on the map twice. The border and selection handles will reappear along with the Map toolbar.

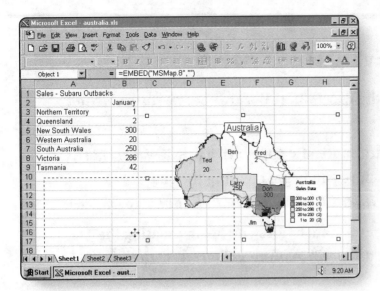

The map feature, like many features in Excel, is fun to use because it surprises you with its power to produce attractive and complex documents so easily. Enjoy!

PART IV REVIEW QUESTIONS

1. How do you access the Excel Chart Wizard? *See the introduction in Chapter 15.*

2. To have your data automatically appear in a preview of a chart, what must you do before you begin creating the chart? *See "Creating a Chart with the Chart Wizard" in Chapter 15.*

3. If you forget to select the data before you begin creating the chart, what can you do? *See "Creating a Chart with the Chart Wizard" in Chapter 15.*

4. What should you do before you can change a label? *See "Improving the Readability of the Chart" in Chapter 15.*

5. In Excel, what is a series? *See the section "Creating a 3-D Bar Chart" in Chapter 16.*

6. In Excel, what is a legend? *See "Creating a 3-D Bar Chart" in Chapter 16.*

7. If you are working with the Chart Wizard, make a mistake, and discover it when you've already left a wizard page, how can you undo your mistake? *See "Creating a 3-D Bar Chart" in Chapter 16.*

8. What are some special effects you can add to your Excel chart? *See "Adding Special Effects" in Chapter 16.*

9. Why is the Excel map feature useful? *See the introduction in Chapter 17.*

10. What must you do to ensure that Excel recognizes that it's working with geographical data? *See "Creating a Map" in Chapter 17.*

PART V

Putting Excel to Work

18 Exploring Functions Further

Excel includes well over 300 functions, some of which you may never use. However, many of the functions can make your daily work with Excel a lot easier. In this chapter, you'll learn how to:

✦ Work with statistical functions

✦ Work with financial functions

WORKING WITH STATISTICAL FUNCTIONS

Statistical functions such as MAXIMUM, MINIMUM, and AVERAGE are very popular in worksheets because they can do much of the number crunching for you. For example, you can figure out the average of a column of numbers by using the AVERAGE function, or you can total a column of numbers by using the SUM function.

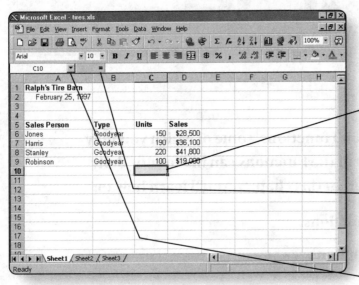

1. **Click** in the **cell** where you want to calculate the average of a column. The cell will become active.

2. **Click** on the **Edit Formula button**. The equal sign will appear in the Formula bar and in the cell you selected.

3. **Click** on the **down arrow** (▼) to the right of the Function box. The Function drop-down list will appear.

4. **Click** on the **function** you want to use.

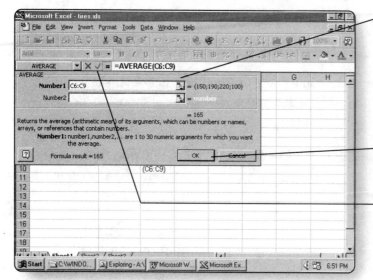

The function dialog box will open—with the preceding cells of the cell you selected entered in the Number1 text box. In this example, the AVERAGE function was selected.

5. **Click** on **OK**. The dialog box will close.

6. **Click** on the **Check Mark (✔) button**. The average will appear in the cell.

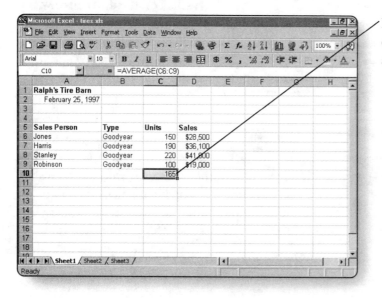

In this example, the average of cells C6 through C9 (165) appears in C10.

WORKING WITH FINANCIAL FUNCTIONS

Excel has some powerful functions that can make working with financial data much easier. One of those functions is *FV* or Future Value.

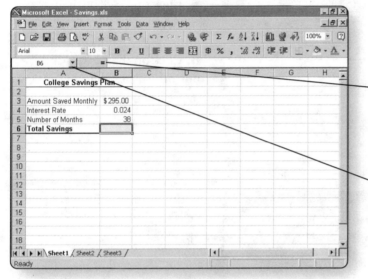

1. Click on the **cell** where you want to enter the function. The cell will become active.

2. Click on the **Edit Formula button**. The equal sign will appear in the Formula bar and in the cell you selected.

3. Click on the **down arrow** (▼) to the right of the Function box. The Function drop-down list will appear.

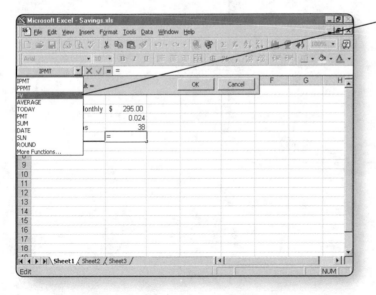

4. Click on the **function** you want to use. The function dialog box will open with text boxes for supplying the necessary data. In this example, FV was selected.

NOTE

If you don't see the function you want to use, click on the down arrow (▼) to the right of Function box. Click on More Functions… and select a function from the Paste Function dialog box.

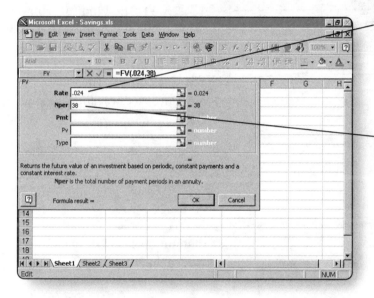

5. **Type** the **interest rate**.

6. **Press** the **Tab key**. The insertion point will move to the Nper text box.

7. **Type** the **number of payments**.

8. **Press** the **Tab key**. The insertion point will move to the Pmt text box.

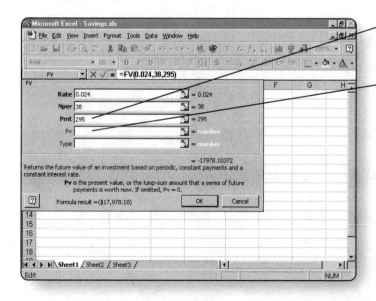

9. **Type** the **amount saved per period**.

10. **Press** the **Tab key**. The insertion point will move to the Pv text box.

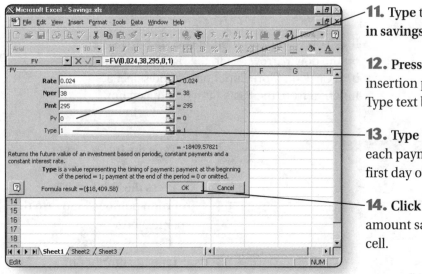

11. Type the **amount currently in savings**.

12. **Press** the **Tab key**. The insertion point will move to the Type text box.

13. **Type 1**. The 1 indicates that each payment is made on the first day of the month.

14. **Click** on **OK**. The total amount saved will appear in the cell.

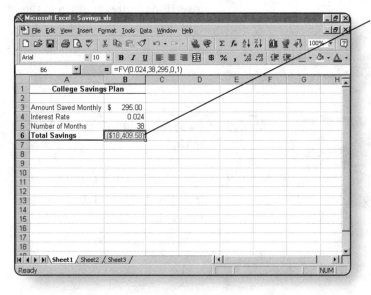

In this example, the total amount saved is $18,409.58. Notice that Excel displays the total as a negative amount because transferring funds to a savings account is a negative cash flow.

19 Creating Depreciation Tables

You can use Excel to calculate the *depreciation*, the reduction in value, of an asset. In this chapter, you'll learn how to:

✦ **Set up a depreciation table**

✦ **Calculate a straight line depreciation amount**

✦ **Calculate a decreasing book value**

MAKING A DEPRECIATION TABLE

A depreciation table determines how much the value of an asset decreases over a set amount a time. You can begin creating the table by typing the labels of the rows.

Setting Up the Table

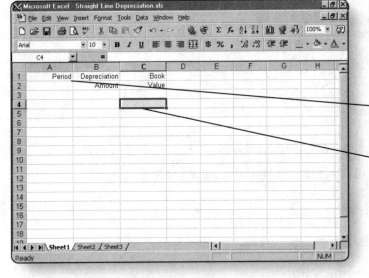

1. Type the **labels** you want to use.

2. Click on **C4**. The cell will be highlighted.

3. Type the **original cost.**

4. Click on the **Check Mark (✔) button**. Excel will accept the value.

Entering the Depreciation Periods

For many assets, the useful life is considered to be ten years. In this example, ten one-year periods are used.

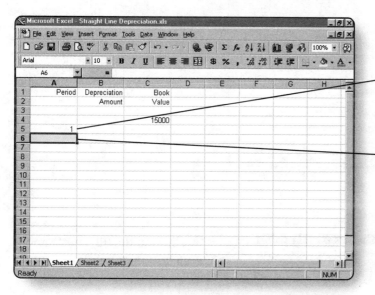

1. **Click** on **A5**. The cell will become active.

2. **Type 1**. In this example, 1 represents the first one-year period.

3. **Press** the **down arrow key.** A6 will become the active cell.

4. **Click** on the **Edit Formula button.** The Formula palette will appear.

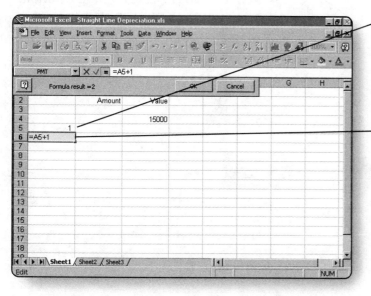

5. **Click** on the **preceding cell.** In this example, A5 was selected. The cell reference A5 will appear in the Formula bar and in the highlighted cell.

6. **Type +1.** +1 will appear in the Formula bar and highlighted cell.

7. **Click** on the **Check Mark (✔) button.** The value in A6 will be increased by one over the preceding cell. In this example, the value 2 will appear.

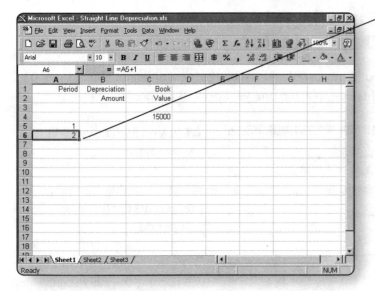

8. Move the **mouse arrow** over the fill handle. The mouse arrow will change to a plus sign.

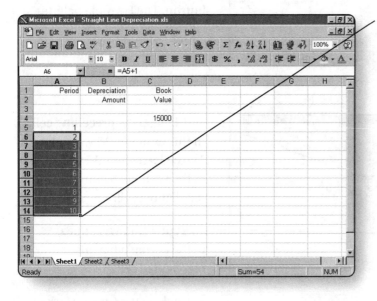

9. Click on the **fill handle** and **drag** it down to select one cell for each period.

10. Release the **mouse button**. Excel will fill the cells with increasing values.

Calculating the Straight Line Depreciation

Straight line depreciation means that the depreciation of an asset is divided equally throughout the periods.

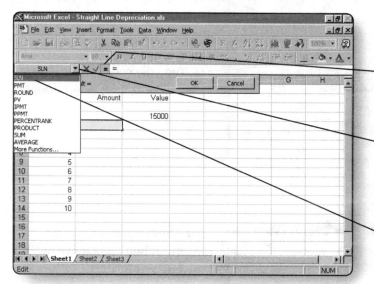

1. **Click** on **B5**. The cell will become active.

2. **Click** on the **Edit Formula button.** The Formula palette will appear.

3. **Click** on the **down arrow (▼)** to the right of the Function box. A drop-down list of functions will appear.

4. **Click** on the **SLN function**. This function calculates straight line depreciation. The SLN dialog box will appear.

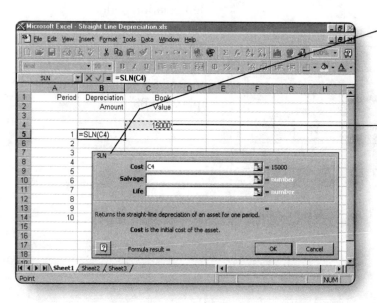

5. **Click** on the **SLN dialog box** and **drag** it down until you can see the total number of periods and the original cost.

6. **Click** on the **cell** containing the original cost. Marching ants will appear around the cell and the cell address will appear in the Cost text box.

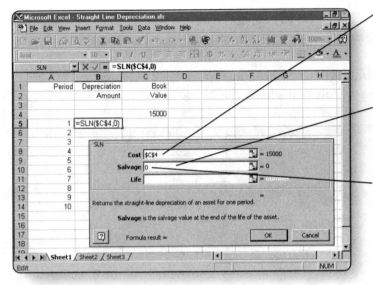

7. Press the **F4 key**. Dollar signs will appear in the cell reference, indicating that this is an absolute reference.

8. Press the **Tab key**. The insertion point will move to the Salvage text box.

9. Type the **value** of the asset at the end of the ten-year period.

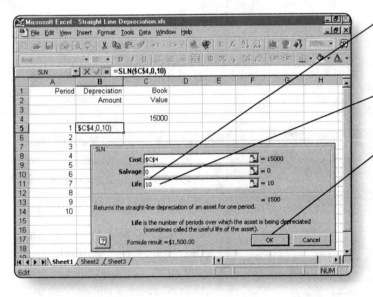

10. Press the **Tab key**. The insertion point will move to the Life text box.

11. Type the **number** of depreciation periods.

12. Click on **OK**. The Straight Line depreciation amount to be used for each period will appear in B5.

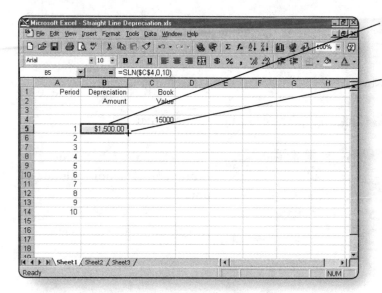

In this example, $1500 is the depreciation amount.

13. **Move** the **mouse pointer** over the fill handle. The pointer will change to a plus sign.

NOTE

Excel automatically formats the straight line depreciation amount as currency.

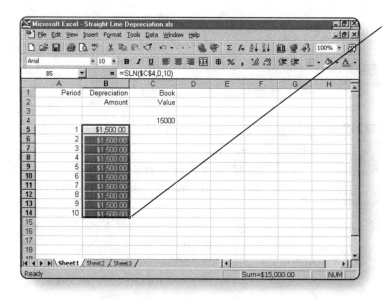

14. **Click** on the **fill handle** and **drag** it down to select one cell for each depreciation period.

15. **Release** the **mouse button**. Excel will fill each of the cells with the same straight line depreciation amount.

Calculating the Book Value for Each Depreciation Period

Now you are ready to calculate the changing depreciation.

1. Click on **C5**. The cell will become active.

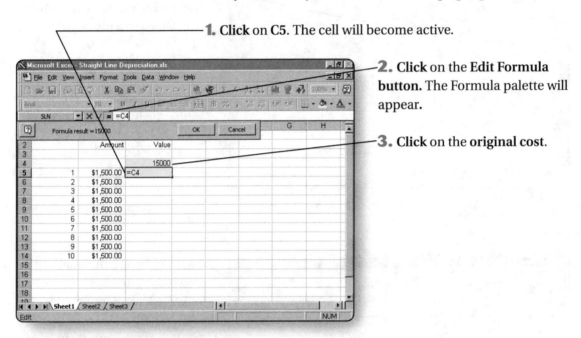

2. Click on the **Edit Formula button.** The Formula palette will appear.

3. Click on the **original cost**.

4. Type -.

5. Click on the **depreciation amount** for the first period.

6. Click on the **Check Mark (✔) button.** The original cost will decrease by the depreciation amount for the first period.

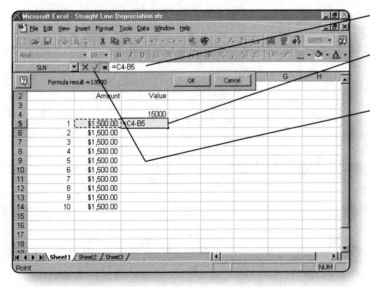

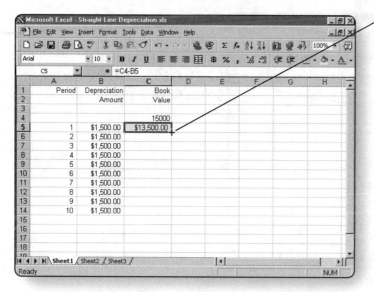

7. Move the **mouse arrow** over the fill handle. The mouse arrow will change to a plus sign.

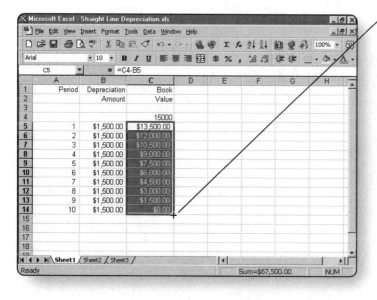

8. **Click** on the **fill handle** and drag it down to select one cell for each depreciation period.

9. **Release** the **mouse button**. Excel will fill each of the cells with the decreasing book value.

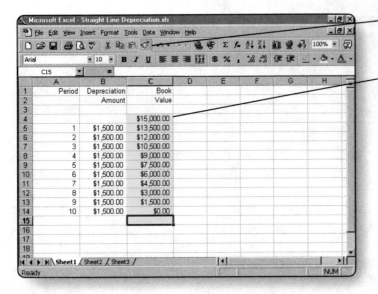

10. Click on the **Format Paintbrush button.**

11. Click on **C4.** Excel will apply the Currency format to that cell.

20 Setting Up Amortization Tables

If you have a loan of $2,000 and you have to pay it off in 10 months, an amortization table can give you some important information. You can use Excel to calculate the interest, principal, and total payment involved in the repayment of the loan. In this chapter, you'll learn how to:

✦ Set up labels for an amortization table

✦ Compute the interest amount of a payment

✦ Determine the principal amount of a payment

✦ Figure out the amount of a payment

✦ Calculate the decreasing balance

CREATING AN AMORTIZATION TABLE

Your table needs four columns for making calculations. You need to calculate how much each payment is, how much of the payment is interest, how much of the payment is principal (and actually reduces the balance), and what the balance is after you make each payment. You also need a fifth column for assigning a number to each payment.

Typing the Labels for a Table

You can begin your amortization table by preparing labels for the columns.

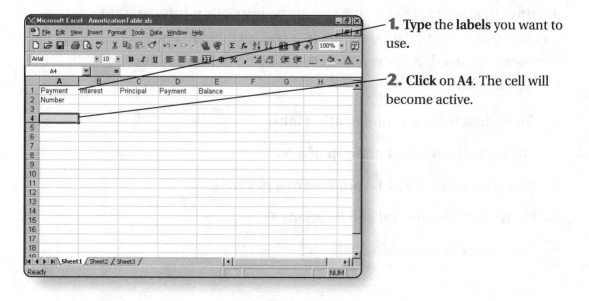

1. **Type** the **labels** you want to use.

2. **Click** on **A4**. The cell will become active.

Setting Up the Column for the Payment Numbers

The first column, Payment Number, assigns a number to each payment.

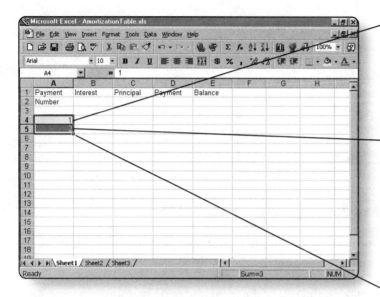

1. Type 1 in the first cell. The number will be entered.

2. Press the Enter key. The next cell in the column will be selected.

3. Type 2 in the second cell.

4. Press the Enter key.

5. Click on the **first cell** and drag the **mouse arrow** across the second. Both cells will be highlighted.

6. Move the **mouse arrow** over the fill handle. The mouse arrow will become a plus sign.

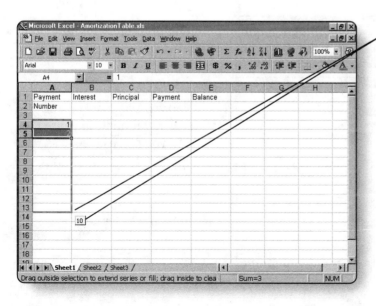

7. Click on the **fill handle** and drag it down until you see a small box containing the number of payments you will be making.

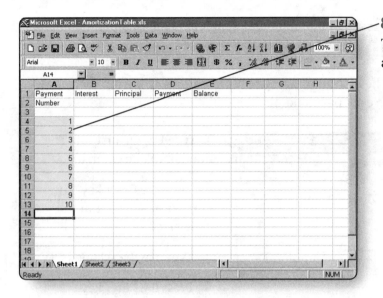

8. **Release** the **mouse button.** The payment numbers will appear in the cells.

Entering the Balance

Before you can calculate the interest per payment, you must place the beginning balance in the Balance column.

1. **Click** on the **cell** in the third row of the Balance column. The cell will become active.

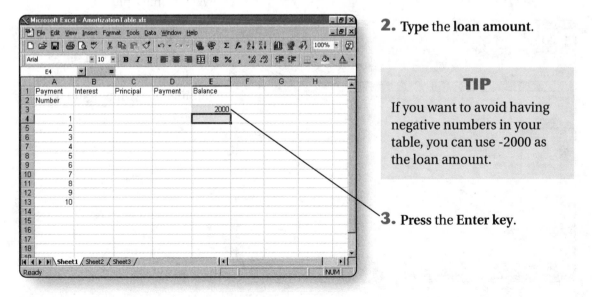

2. **Type** the **loan amount.**

TIP

If you want to avoid having negative numbers in your table, you can use -2000 as the loan amount.

3. **Press** the **Enter key.**

Calculating the Interest Amount of a Payment

Now you are ready to calculate the amount of your payment eaten up by interest.

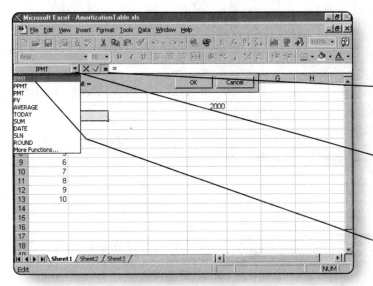

1. Click on the **cell** in the fourth row of the Interest column. The cell will become active.

2. Click on the **Edit Formula button.** The Formula palette will open.

3. Click on the **down arrow** (▼) to the right of the Function box. A drop-down list of functions will appear.

4. Click on **IPMT.** The IPMT function dialog box will open.

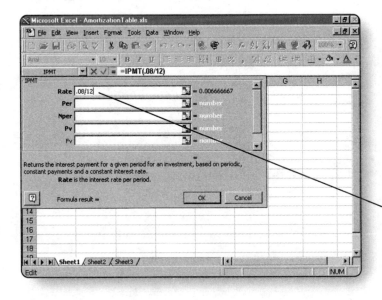

NOTE

If you don't see the function you want to use, click on the down arrow (▼) to the right of Function box. Click on More Functions… and select a function from the Paste Function dialog box.

5. Type the **interest rate divided by 12** in the Rate text box.

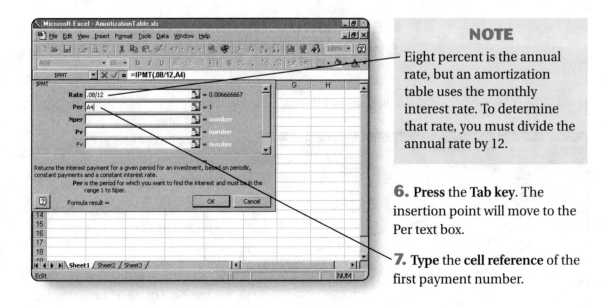

Eight percent is the annual rate, but an amortization table uses the monthly interest rate. To determine that rate, you must divide the annual rate by 12.

6. **Press** the **Tab key**. The insertion point will move to the Per text box.

7. **Type** the **cell reference** of the first payment number.

8. **Press** the **Tab key**. The insertion point will move to the Nper text box.

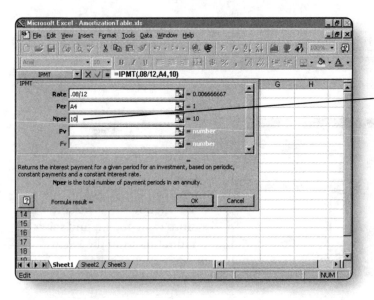

9. **Type** the **number of periods**.

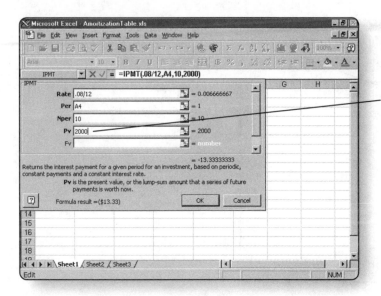

10. Press the **Tab key**. The insertion point will move to the Pv text box.

11. Type the **beginning balance**.

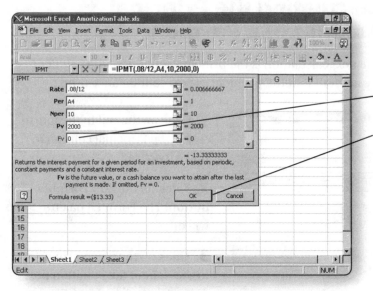

12. Press the **Tab key**. The insertion point will move to the Fv text box.

13. Type the **ending balance**.

14. Click on **OK**. The IPMT dialog box will close.

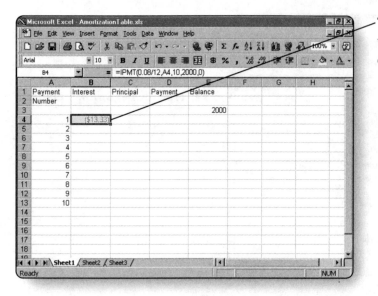

The interest amount, $13.33 in this example, will appear in the cell.

Calculating the Principal Amount of a Payment

The next calculation is the principal amount of the payment—the amount that the payment makes your balance drop.

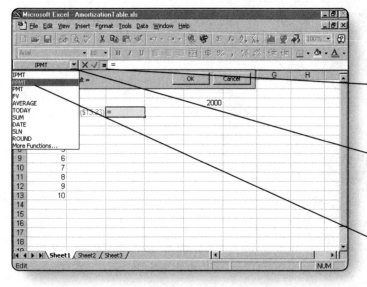

1. **Click** on the **cell** in the fourth row of the Principal column to make it active.

2. **Click** on the **Edit Formula button.** The Formula palette will open.

3. **Click** on the **down arrow** (▼) to the right of the Function box. A drop-down list of functions will appear.

4. **Click** on **PPMT.** The PPMT function dialog box will appear.

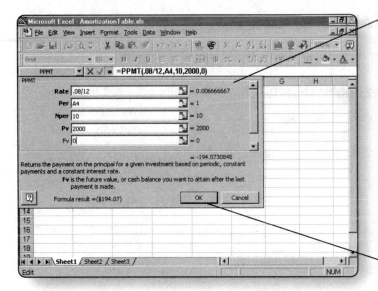

5. **Type data** in the PPMT function dialog box. The data will be entered.

NOTE

The data for this dialog box is the same as the information entered in the IPMT function dialog box in "Calculating the Interest Amount of a Payment."

6. **Click** on **OK**. The PPMT function dialog box will close.

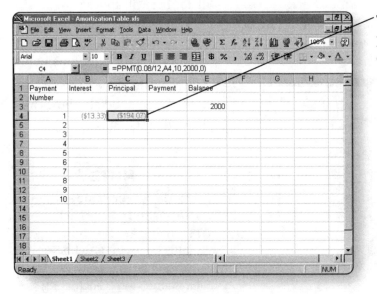

The principal amount of the payment, $194.07 in this example, will appear.

Entering the Payment Amount

Next, you enter the payment amount in the Payment column.

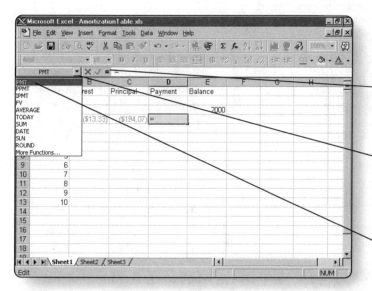

1. Click on the **cell** in the fourth row of the Payment column. The cell will become active.

2. Click on the **Edit Formula button.** The Formula palette will open.

3. Click on the **down arrow (▼)** to the right of the Function box. The drop-down list of functions will appear.

4. Click on **PMT**. The PMT dialog box will appear.

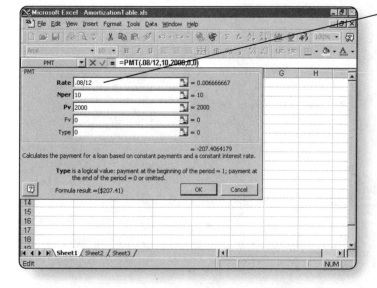

5. Type data in the first four lines of the PMT dialog box. The data will be entered.

NOTE

This data is the same as the information entered in the preceding two function dialog boxes in "Calculating the Interest Amount of a Payment" and "Calculating the Principal Amount of a Payment." However, the Per text box is missing.

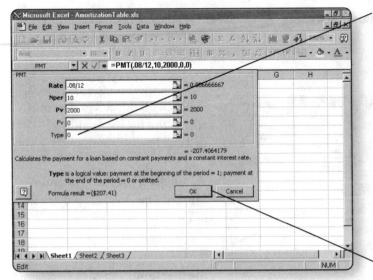

6. Type a **number** in the Type text box.

TIP

Type refers to when the payment is made. If you make a payment the day you borrow the money, the loan is Type 1. If you make a payment one month (or period) after you borrow the money, the loan is Type 0.

7. Click on **OK**. The PMT dialog box will close.

The payment amount, $207.41 in this example, will appear.

NOTE

Since Excel rounds each individual calculation to two decimal places, the Interest and Principal amounts sometimes do not equal the Payment amount that Excel displays.

Calculating the Decreasing Balance

In this column, you begin to see the results of all that outgoing money.

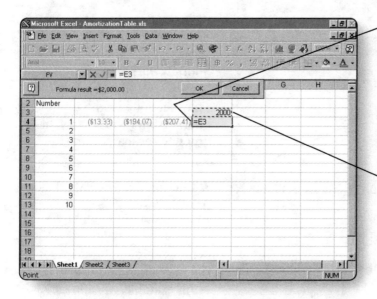

1. Click on the **cell** in the fourth row in the Balance column. The cell will become active.

2. Click on the **Edit Formula button**. The Formula palette will open.

3. Click on the **cell containing the beginning balance**. Marching ants will appear around the cell.

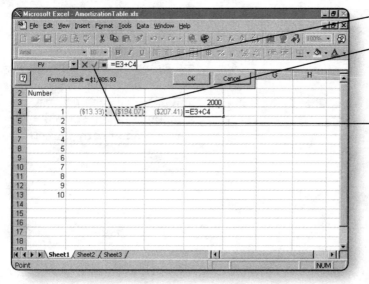

4. Type +.

5. Click on the **cell containing the principal**. Marching ants will appear around the cell.

6. Click on the **Check Mark (✔) button**. The formula will be entered.

TIP

If you open a menu but don't want to make a selection, simply click anywhere on the screen outside of the menu box and the menu will close.

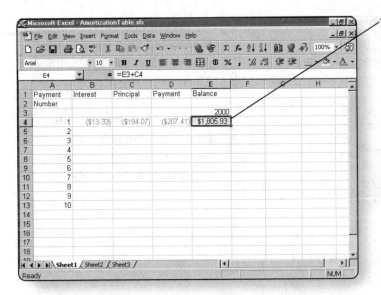

The new balance, $1805.93 in this example, will appear.

COPYING THE FORMULAS DOWN THE WORKSHEET

Now that you've taken the time to enter the formulas in the first calculated row of the worksheet, you can just copy the formulas down the rest of the worksheet.

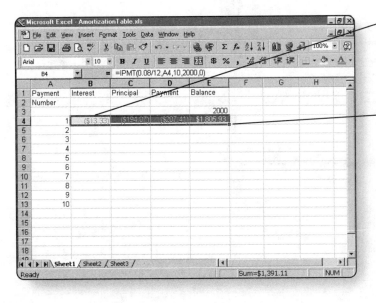

1. **Click** on a **cell** and **drag** with the **mouse arrow** across the range of data to be copied. The range will be highlighted.

2. **Click** on the **fill handle.** Excel will copy the contents of the range to the Clipboard.

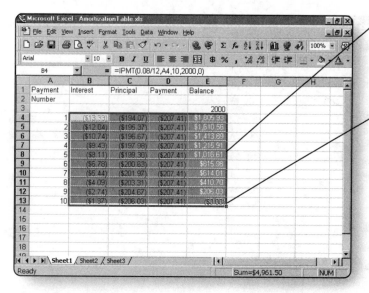

3. **Press** and **hold** the **mouse button** and **drag** down until you reach the last payment number. The cells will be highlighted.

4. **Release** the **mouse button**. Excel will fill the cells with the data resulting from the copied formulas.

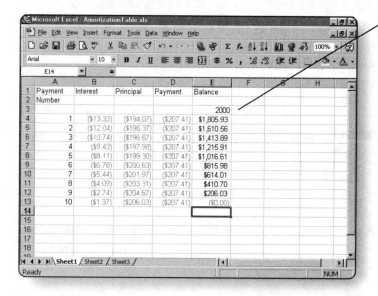

5. **Click outside** of the selected range. Excel will remove the highlighting so that you can see the completed amortization table.

21 Integrating Excel with Word

Excel and Word work together smoothly so you can combine an Excel worksheet with a Word document easily. For example, you can have a memo created in Word that contains an Excel worksheet. In this chapter, you'll learn how to:

✦ Create an Excel worksheet from within Word

✦ Format a new Excel worksheet

✦ Insert rows or columns in a new Excel worksheet

✦ Insert an existing Excel worksheet into a Word document

CREATING AN EXCEL WORK-SHEET FROM WITHIN WORD

One way to get an Excel worksheet into a Word document is to cut and paste it. That method involves first creating the worksheet in Excel, copying it, and then pasting it into a Word document. But you can create an Excel worksheet in a Word document without having to create the worksheet in Excel first.

You can create an Excel worksheet right in a Word document by using the Insert Microsoft Excel Worksheet button. The worksheet you create is actually part of the Word document and when you save the Word file this spreadsheet is saved as part of the document. This is called *embedding* a worksheet in Word.

1. **Type text** in the Word document.

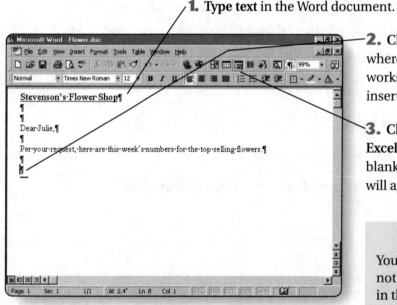

2. **Click** in the **Word document** where you want your Excel worksheet to appear. The insertion point will be placed.

3. **Click** on the **Insert Microsoft Excel Worksheet button.** A blank Excel worksheet palette will appear.

NOTE

Your Word document may not look exactly like the one in the figure. The appearance of the document will depend on the options you have chosen, the template you are using, and any formatting you may have done to the document.

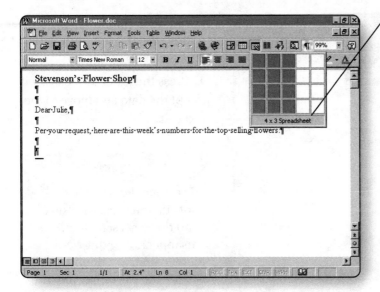

4. **Move** the **mouse arrow** over the palette until you see the number of columns and rows you want at the bottom of the palette.

5. **Click** on the **spreadsheet style** you want to use.

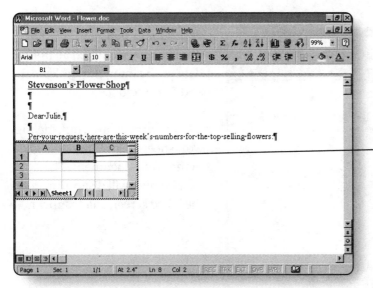

6. **Press** the **Enter key.** An Excel screen containing a worksheet, menu bar, and toolbar will appear within the Word document, but the Microsoft Word title bar will remain.

7. **Click** in the **cell** where you want to enter data. Excel will highlight the cell with a dark border.

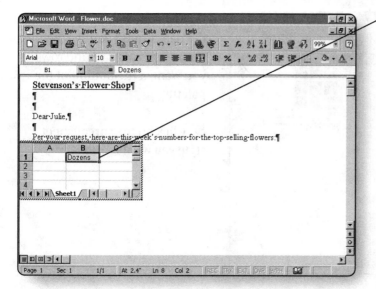

8. **Enter** the **data** you want to appear in that cell.

9. **Press** the **Enter key.** Excel will accept the data and move to the next cell.

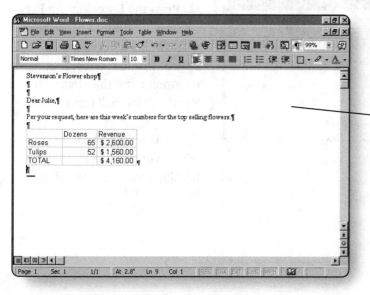

10. **Repeat steps 7** through **9** until you have entered all the data you want in the worksheet and formatted it.

11. **Click** on an **area** outside the worksheet to see how it will look in the Word document. The Excel screen will disappear, and the Word screen will reappear.

Formatting the New Excel Worksheet

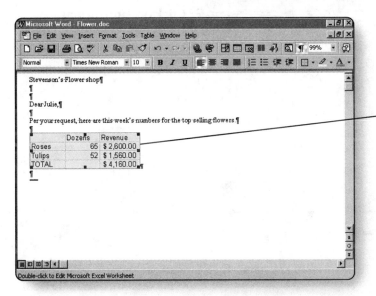

You can change the number category, font, and alignment of the Excel worksheet, using the Excel Format menu.

1. **Click** in the **Excel worksheet.** Selection handles will appear around the worksheet.

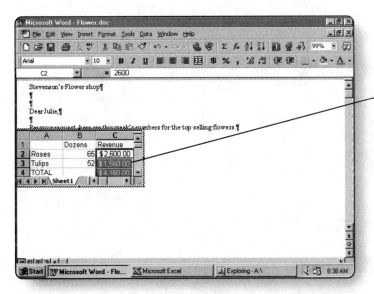

2. **Click** in the **Excel worksheet** again. The Excel window will appear.

3. **Click** on any **cells** in the worksheet. The cells will become active.

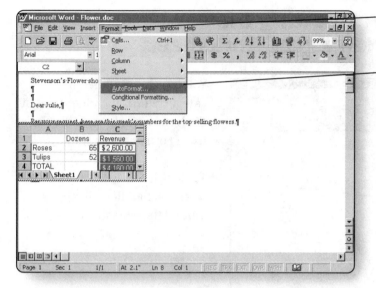

4. **Click** on **Format**. The Format menu will appear.

5. **Click** on **AutoFormat**. The AutoFormat dialog box will open.

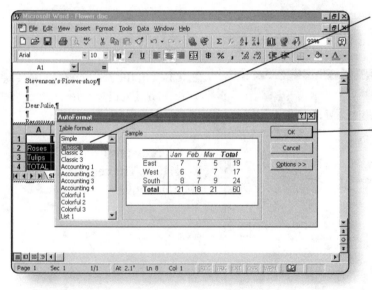

6. **Click** on a **format** in the Table format: text box that you want to use. A sample of that format will appear in the Sample box.

7. **Click** on **OK**. The AutoFormat dialog box will close.

NOTE
Your worksheet may not exactly match the one in the figure.

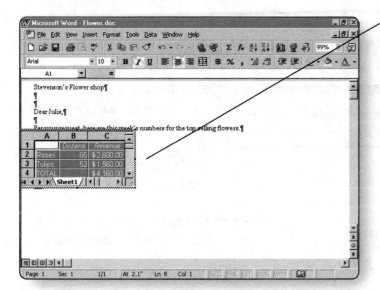

8. Click on an **area** outside the worksheet to see how it will look in the Word document. The Excel screen will disappear, and the Word screen will appear with the formatted Excel worksheet.

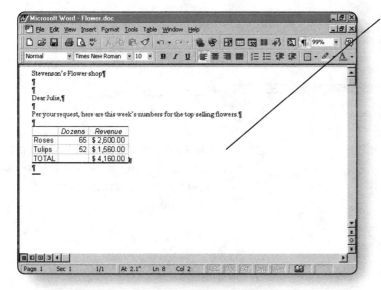

The worksheet will appear in the format that you chose.

TIP

If only part of your worksheet appears, click inside the worksheet. The Excel screen will reappear. Scroll to the top of the worksheet, press and hold the mouse button and drag the lower right corner of the worksheet until you can see the entire worksheet, and then click on an area outside the worksheet. The entire worksheet will appear in the Word document.

Inserting Rows or Columns in the Excel Worksheet

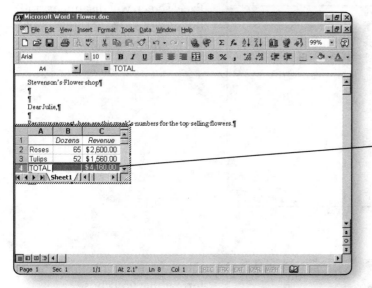

If you forget a row or column, you can use the Excel window to insert the missing element.

1. **Click** in the **Excel worksheet**. The Excel window will appear.

2. **Click** in the **cells** where you want the new element to appear.

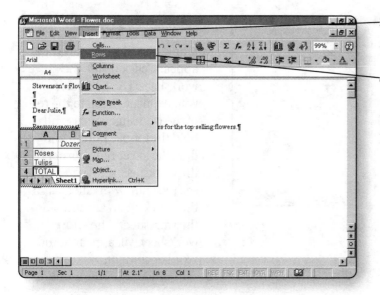

3. **Click** on **Insert**. The Insert menu will appear.

4. **Click** on the **Row** or **Column**, depending on the element that you want to insert into the worksheet.

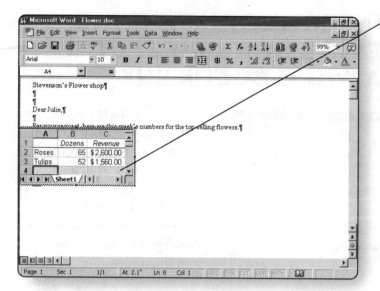

The new row or column will be inserted.

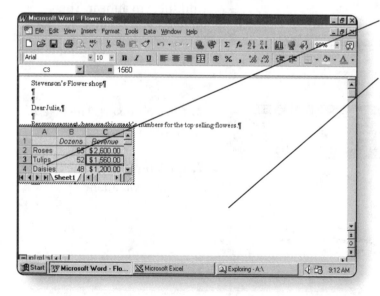

5. **Enter** the **data** that is missing.

6. **Click outside** of the Excel worksheet. You will now be able to continue typing and complete the Word document.

INSERTING AN EXISTING EXCEL WORKSHEET INTO A WORD DOCUMENT

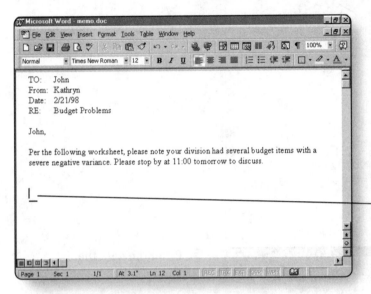

You also can insert existing Excel worksheets into Word documents, embedding the worksheets or linking them. *Linking files* means that changes you make in the worksheet in the Excel file also appear in the Word file that contains the Excel worksheet.

1. Click in the **Word document** where you want your Excel worksheet to appear. The insertion point will be placed.

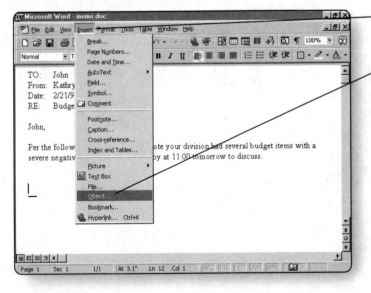

2. Click on **Insert**. The Insert menu will appear.

3. Click on **Object**. The Object dialog box will open.

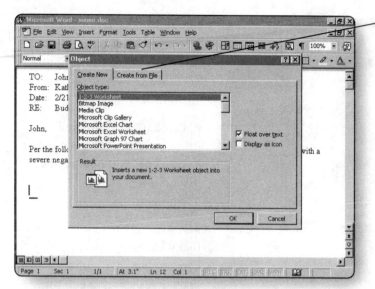

4. Click on the **Create from File tab**. The tab will come to the front.

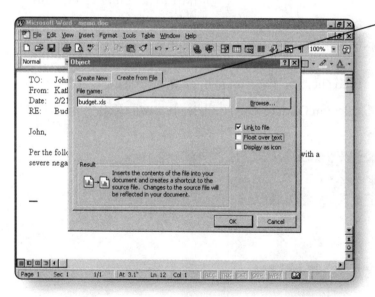

5. Type the **filename** of the Excel worksheet in the File name: text box.

NOTE

If you can't remember the filename, use the Browse button.

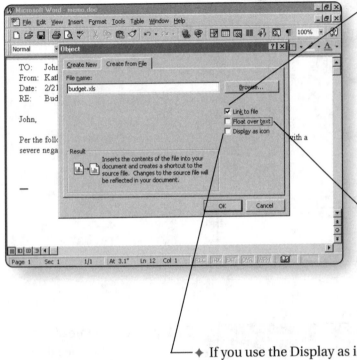

6. Click on each of the following **check box options** that you want to use with this worksheet. A ✔ will appear, if the item was selected.

♦ If you use the Link to file option, the worksheet in the Word document changes whenever the Excel file changes.

♦ If you use the Float over text option, you can edit the worksheet in Excel, but changes you make to the Excel file aren't made to the Word document containing the worksheet.

♦ If you use the Display as icon option, an icon will appear in your Word document, not the actual worksheet. The reader then clicks on the icon to open the worksheet.

7. Click on **OK**. The Object dialog box will close.

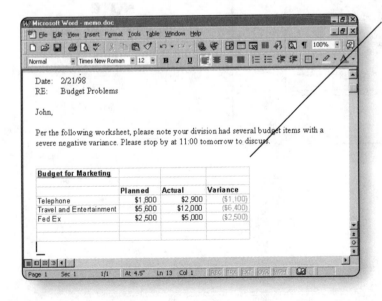

The Excel worksheet will appear in the Word document.

CHECKING WHETHER A LINK IS WORKING PROPERLY

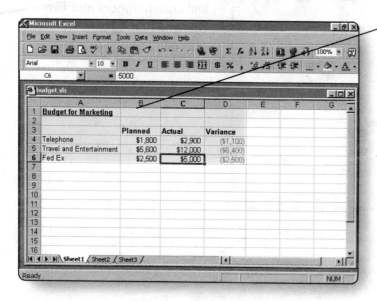

1. **Open** the **Excel file** containing the worksheet linked to a Word document.

2. **Make** a **change** in the worksheet. In this example, the Travel and Entertainment actual figure was changed from $12,000 to $14,000.

3. **Click** on the **Excel Minimize button.** The window will be minimized.

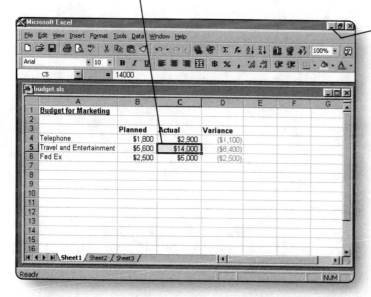

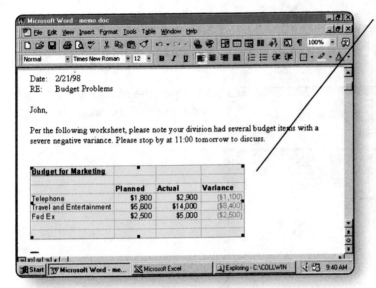

The Word window will appear with the change in data reflected. Notice that the travel and entertainment number changed from $12,000 to $14,000!

PART V REVIEW QUESTIONS

1. **What are some of the statistical functions that Excel offers?** *See "Working with Statistical Functions" in Chapter 18.*

2. **How can you use the FV function in your finances?** *See "Working with Financial Functions" in Chapter 18.*

3. **What does the term "depreciation" mean?** *See the introduction in Chapter 19.*

4. **What function calculates straight line depreciation?** *See "Calculating the Straight Line Depreciation" in Chapter 19.*

5. **What information does an amortization table provide?** *See the introduction in Chapter 20.*

6. **What functions calculate the interest, principal, and payment amounts of a loan?** *See the introduction in Chapter 20.*

7. **What is an advantage to having a word processing program and a spreadsheet program that are compatible?** *See the introduction in Chapter 21.*

8. **What limitations does embedding an object within a document create?** *See "Creating an Excel Worksheet from within Word" in Chapter 21.*

9. **How can you quickly create an Excel worksheet within a Word document?** *See "Creating an Excel Worksheet from within Word" in Chapter 21.*

10. **What does the term "linking" files mean?** *See "Inserting an Existing Excel Worksheet into a Word Document" in Chapter 23.*

PART VI
Getting Online with Excel

22 Getting Help on the Web

Nearly everywhere you turn you hear the phrase "World Wide Web." Excel 97 includes an option on its Help menu for accessing the World Wide Web. This chapter assumes that you have an Internet Service Provider and connect to the Web using Internet Explorer. In this chapter, you'll learn how to:

✦ Use the Web tutorial

✦ Get answers to frequently asked questions

✦ Search for technical support information

✦ Explore Microsoft's free stuff page

ACCESSING THE WEB TUTORIAL

The Excel Help menu offers an option for accessing a tutorial about the Internet—and the World Wide Web, specifically. You can access that tutorial through the Microsoft on the Web option.

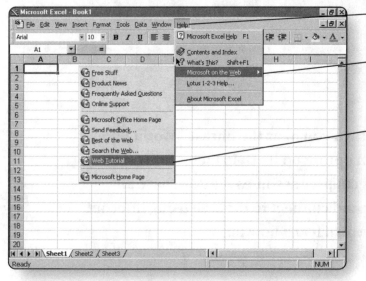

1. **Click** on **Help.** The Help menu will appear.

2. **Click** on **Microsoft on the Web.** The Microsoft on the Web submenu will appear.

3. **Click** on **Web Tutorial.** The Internet Explorer window will open and a Connect To dialog box may appear.

TIP

Each choice on this menu connects you to a location on Microsoft's Web site.

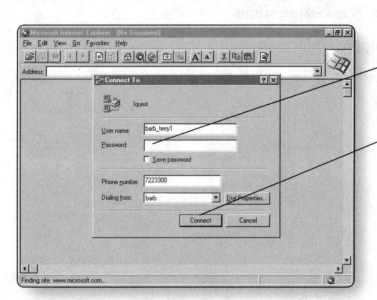

4. **Type** your **password** in the Connect To dialog box, if necessary.

5. **Click** on **Connect.** After the connection is made, a Web tutorial will appear.

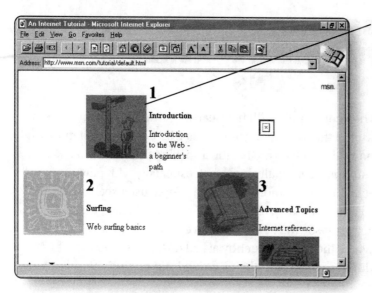

6. Click on a **topic**, depending on your computer skills. A Web tutorial will appear.

7. Complete the **tutorial**.

8. Complete **one** of the **following actions** when you have finished as much of the tutorial as you want:

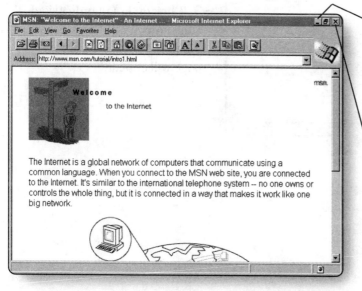

✦ Click on the **Minimize button**. Internet Explorer will be minimized. You can now click on another Microsoft on the Web option from the Excel Help menu.

✦ Click on the **Close button**. The session will end and Internet Explorer will close.

GETTING ANSWERS TO FREQUENTLY ASKED QUESTIONS

When confronted with new learning situations, people often assume that they're the only ones who don't understand something or who are having a specific problem. That assumption is usually incorrect, especially with new technologies. As more and more people use Excel, the same old questions keep coming up—so often, in fact, that Microsoft software sites now have areas set up specifically to answer the most frequently asked questions. Microsoft has added that option to their Getting Help on the Web submenu.

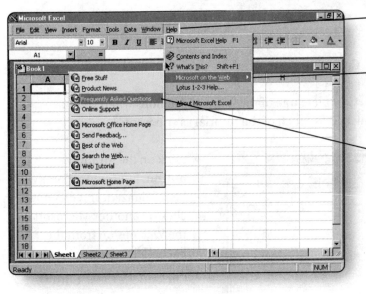

1. **Click** on **Help.** The Help menu will appear.

2. **Click** on **Microsoft on the Web.** The Microsoft on the Web submenu will appear.

3. **Click** on **Frequently Asked Questions.** The Microsoft Excel Frequently Asked Questions page will appear.

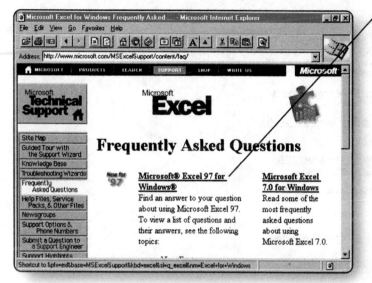

4. **Click** on an **underlined link**. The Excel Frequently Asked Questions Table of Contents page will appear.

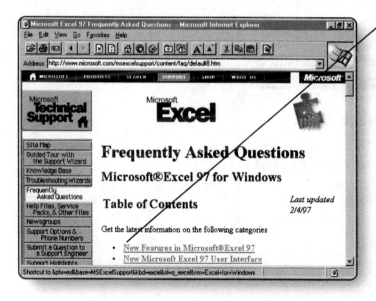

5. **Click** on another **underlined link**. A new page listing questions will appear.

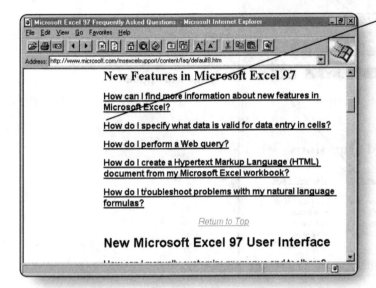

6. **Click** on a **question**. A new page with the answer to that question will appear.

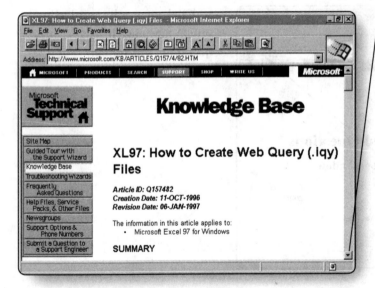

7. **Click** on the **down scroll arrow** to read the entire answer.

8. Complete one of the **following actions**:

✦ **Click** on the **Back arrow**. You will return to the Frequently Asked Questions page.

✦ **Click** on the **Minimize button** (⬜). Internet Explorer will minimize and you can maximize Excel to choose another Microsoft on the Web option.

✦ **Click** on the **Close button** (☒). The session will end and Internet Explorer will close.

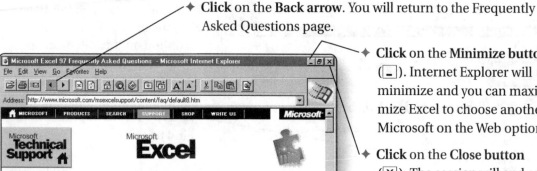

SEARCHING FOR TECHNICAL SUPPORT INFORMATION

If you can't find the answer to your question on the Microsoft Frequently Asked Questions page, you can conduct your own search for answers from the Microsoft Web site. If you still don't find an answer, you can use Online Support, but you will be charged for this service.

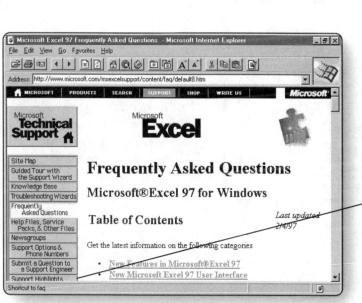

1. Click on **Support Highlights** on the Frequently Asked Questions page. The Support Highlights page will appear.

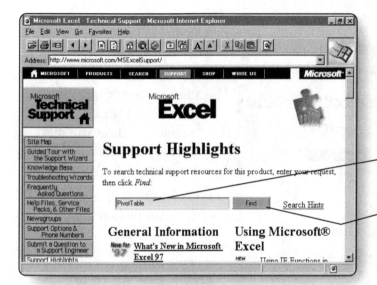

2. Type a **word or phrase** in the Find text box.

3. Click on **Find**. A Find Results page listing a portion of the findings for the word you typed will appear.

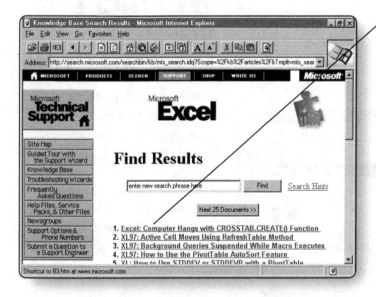

4. Click on an **underlined link**. A Knowledge Base page displaying information will appear.

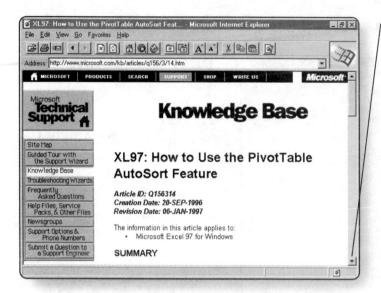

5. Click on the **down scroll arrow** to read the answer.

6. Complete one of the following actions:

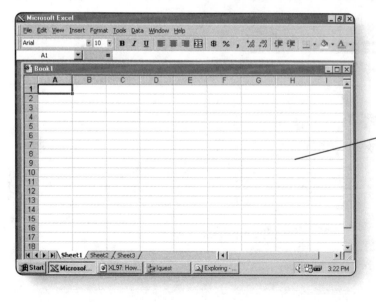

✦ Click on the **Back arrow** to return to the page listing the findings. Continue clicking on links and reading pages or enter another topic in the Find text box.

✦ Click on the **Minimize button**. Internet Explorer will minimize and Excel will reappear. You can now choose another Microsoft on the Web option from the Excel Help menu.

✦ Click on the **Close button**. The session will end and Internet Explorer will close.

SEARCHING FOR FREE STUFF

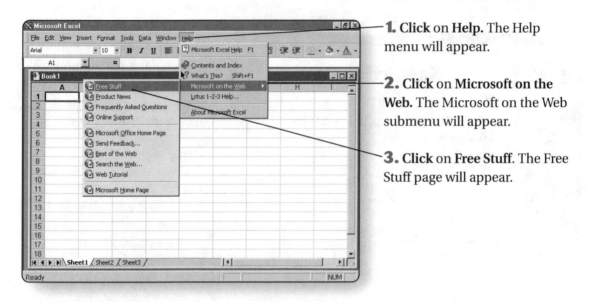

1. Click on **Help.** The Help menu will appear.

2. Click on **Microsoft on the Web.** The Microsoft on the Web submenu will appear.

3. Click on **Free Stuff**. The Free Stuff page will appear.

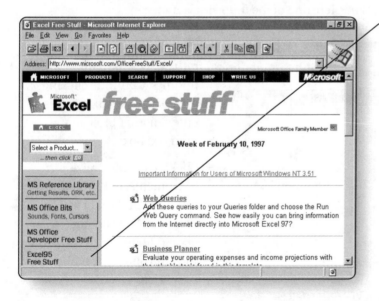

4. Click on a **link**. A new page will appear.

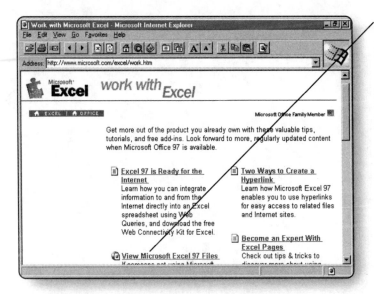

5. **Click** on another **link.** A new page will appear.

6. **Continue exploring** the **Web** for as long as you want for free stuff.

23 Using Excel in a Web Page

The World Wide Web has become very popular in the last 2 years. Sharing data on the Web is incredibly easy, and one way is to use an Excel worksheet in a Web page. Microsoft has made this very easy to do in Excel 97. In this chapter, you'll learn how to:

✦ Save an Excel worksheet as a Web page

✦ View an Excel worksheet Web page

SAVING THE WORKSHEET FOR THE WEB

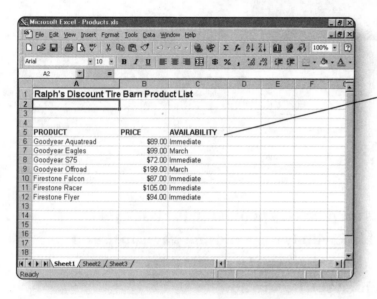

One way you can use a Web page is to let customers know the availability of products.

1. **Type text** for the Excel worksheet.

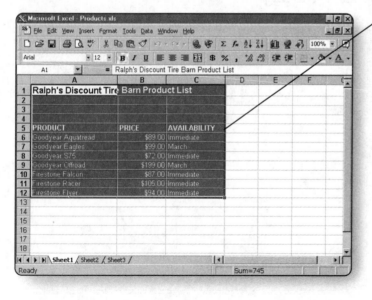

2. **Click** on a **cell** and **drag** across the range you want to save. The cells will be highlighted.

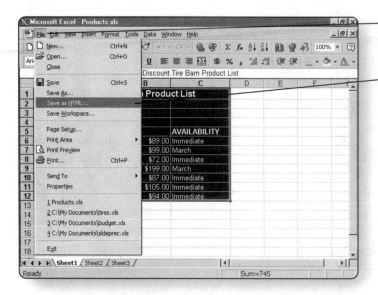

3. **Click** on **File**. The File menu will appear.

4. **Click** on **Save as HTML**. The Internet Assistant Wizard – Step 1 of 4 dialog box will open with the highlighted range in the Ranges and charts to convert: text box.

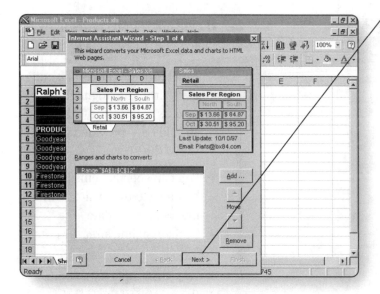

5. **Click** on **Next**. The Internet Assistant Wizard – Step 2 of 4 dialog box will open.

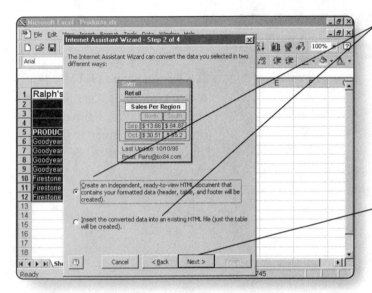

6. **Click** on one of the following **options**:

✦ The first option, the default, creates a separate HTML document.

✦ The second option places the worksheet in an existing HTML file.

7. **Click** on **Next.** The Internet Assistant Wizard – Step 3 of 4 dialog box will open.

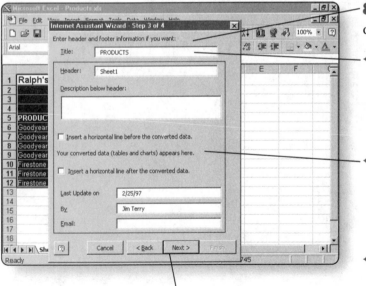

8. **Fill out** the text boxes in the dialog box.

✦ Excel provides an intelligent guess from the highlighted cells as to what the Title should be—provided you've saved the file.

✦ You can specify to insert a header, a footer, a horizontal line before the data, or a horizontal line after the data.

✦ You can supply data about the creator of the HTML document and the date it was created.

9. **Click** on **Next.** The Internet Assistant Wizard – Step 4 of 4 dialog box will open.

10. **Fill out** the text boxes in the dialog box.

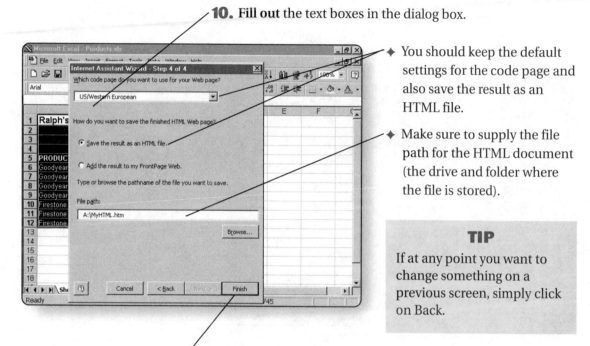

◆ You should keep the default settings for the code page and also save the result as an HTML file.

◆ Make sure to supply the file path for the HTML document (the drive and folder where the file is stored).

TIP

If at any point you want to change something on a previous screen, simply click on Back.

11. **Click** on **Finish.** Excel will save the worksheet as an HTML document that can load on any Web page.

VIEWING THE EXCEL WORKSHEET HTML DOCUMENT

After you create the HTML document, you should make sure that it is correct. A simple way to view the HTML document is to use the Windows Explorer and open the file.

1. **Click** on **Start** from the Windows desktop. The Start menu will appear.

2. **Click** on **Programs**. The Programs menu will appear.

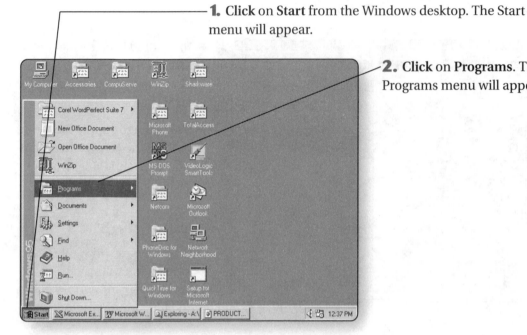

3. **Click** on **Windows Explorer.** The Windows Explorer window will appear.

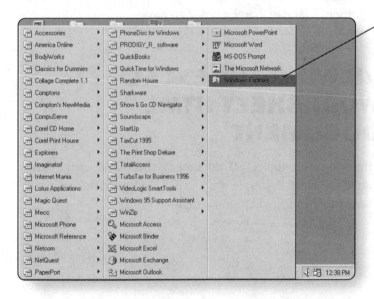

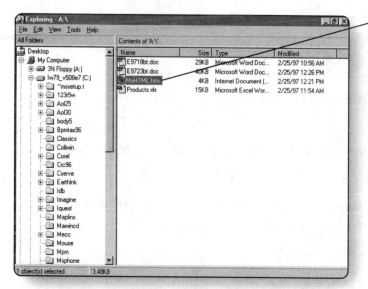

4. **Find** your **HTML file.** It will be in the drive and folder identified in the Internet Assistant. The file will have an HTM extension.

5. **Click twice** on the **filename.**

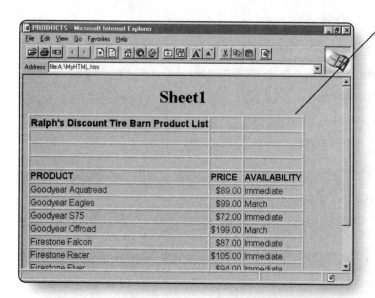

The file will open and your Excel worksheet should look like a Web page.

PART VI REVIEW QUESTIONS

1. How can you learn about the Web? *See the introduction in Chapter 22.*

2. What dialog box may open before you can access the Microsoft Web site? *See "Accessing the Web Tutorial" in Chapter 22.*

3. Where should you begin looking for an answer if you have a question about the Web? *See "Getting Answers to Frequently Asked Questions" in Chapter 22.*

4. What happens if you click on text that is underlined or a different color on a Web page? *See "Getting Answers to Frequently Asked Questions" in Chapter 22.*

5. In addition to the Frequently Asked Questions section, which Help option can you use to search for technical support? *See "Searching for Technical Support Information" in Chapter 22.*

6. What is a search engine? *See "Searching for Technical Support Information" in Chapter 22.*

7. What is one way you can use Excel on the Web? *See "Saving the Worksheet on the Web" in Chapter 23.*

8. What must you do before you save a worksheet as an HTML document? *See "Saving the Worksheet on the Web" in Chapter 23.*

9. What are the two ways you can save an Excel worksheet as an HTML document? *See "Saving the Worksheet on the Web" in Chapter 23.*

10. How can you see what your Web page will look like? *See "Viewing the Excel Worksheet HTML Document" in Chapter 23.*

PART VII

Using an Excel Template

Using the Expense Statement Template

The Expense Statement workbook template is used when you want to create a workbook to keep track of personal expenses, such as those you might incur during a business trip. The Expense Statement template provides places for you to insert expenses relating to accommodations, transportation, fuel, meals, phone charges, entertainment, and other items. In this appendix, you will learn how to:

✦ Create and customize a new Expense Statement workbook template

✦ Insert data and a logo in the template

✦ Change worksheet fonts in the template

✦ Use the Expense toolbar

CREATING AN EXPENSE STATEMENT WORKBOOK TEMPLATE

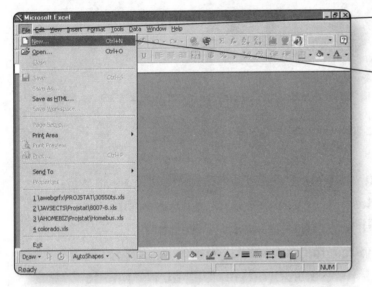

1. Click on **File**. The File menu will appear.

2. Click on **New**. The New dialog box will open.

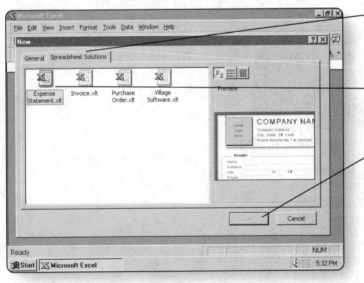

3. Click on the **Spreadsheet Solutions tab**. The tab will come to the front.

4. Click on the **Expense Statement icon**. The icon will be highlighted.

5. Click on **OK**. A Microsoft Excel dialog box will open.

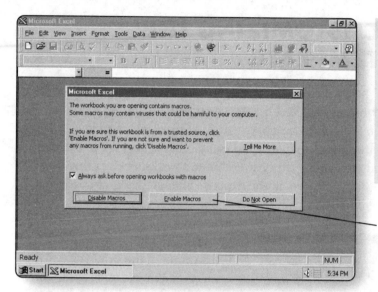

NOTE

If you do not see the Expense Statement workbook template in the New dialog box, you will need to install this template from your Microsoft Office 97 or Microsoft Excel 97 CD-ROM or disks.

6. Click on **Enable Macros**. The dialog box will close.

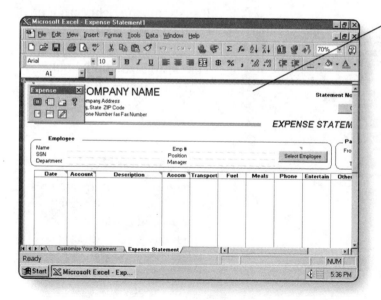

The Expense Statement workbook template will open in the Excel window.

CUSTOMIZING THE TEMPLATE

When the Expense Statement workbook template opens, it contains two worksheets. The top worksheet, Expense Statement, is the worksheet you fill out with employee information, expense data, and other information. You can customize the Expense Statement worksheet by using the other worksheet in the Expense Statement workbook template, named "Customizing Your Statement."

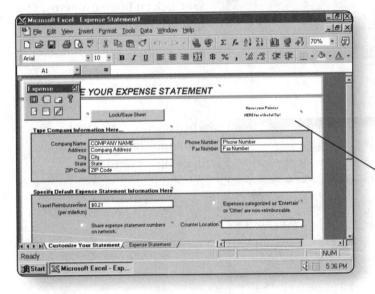

1. Click on the **Customize button** on the Expense Statement worksheet. You might need to scroll to the right side of the worksheet to see this button. It sits at the top right corner of the worksheet.

The Customize Your Statement worksheet will be displayed.

NOTE

The text items in the gray shaded area are the labels for each field that appear on the Expense Statement worksheet.

Filling Out Company Information

On the Customize Your Statement worksheet, you can insert your company information so that each time you open a new Expense Statement worksheet, your company information will appear at the top of the worksheet.

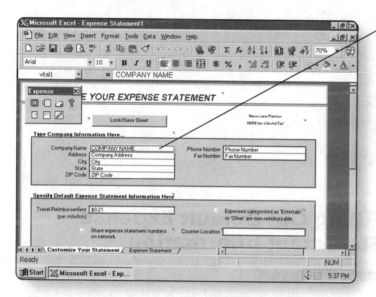

1. Click in the **Company Name cell.** The insertion point will be placed.

2. Type the **name** of your company in this text box. The text, COMPANY NAME, will be replaced.

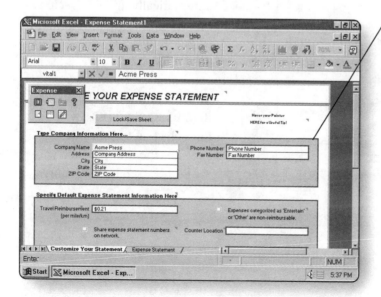

3. Repeat steps 1 and **2** for the rest of the cells (Address, City, State, ZIP CODE, Phone Number, and Fax Number) in the Type Company Information Here... box.

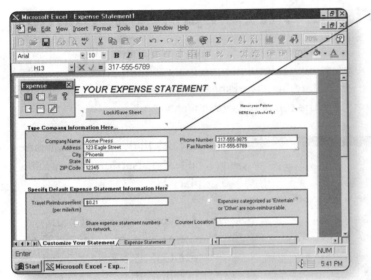

Here's an example of how the company information area looks with customized data inserted.

Filling Out Default Expense Statement Information

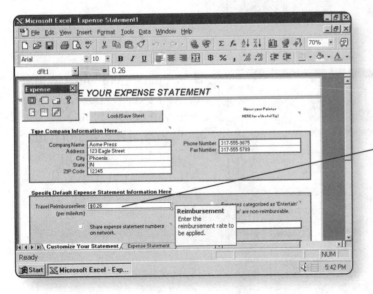

The default expense statement information is used to automatically update specific cells in the Expense Statement worksheet each time you fill in the worksheet.

1. Click in the **Travel Reimbursement cell**. By default, this cell is set to $0.21, which specifies the rate at which you are reimbursed for each mile.

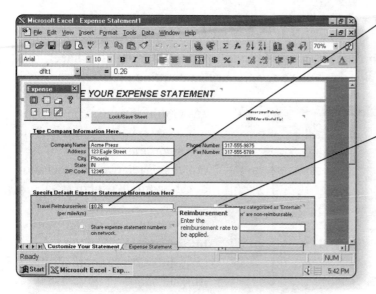

2. Type your **company's rate**, if it is different. If your company does not reimburse per mile, delete the data in this cell so it is empty.

3. Click in the **Expenses categorized as 'Entertain' or 'Other' are non-reimbursable** check box. There will be columns called "Entertainment" and "Other" in your worksheet which will not be calculated in total reimbursed expenses.

NOTE

If you do not want to use this option, remove the ✔ by clicking on the item again.

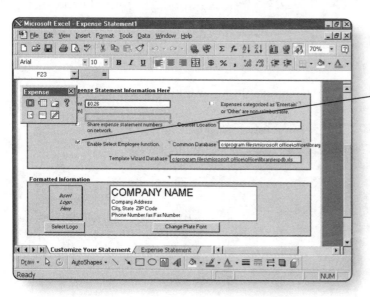

4. Click on the **Enable Select Employee**. This will disable a feature that lets you pick employee names and other employee data from a database. This option is useful only if you intend to share this template file with other users, such as on a network.

Inserting a Logo

You can add a logo to your Expense Statement worksheet. This helps dress up your worksheet and further personalizes it for your company. You can specify any graphic image to be inserted as a logo on your worksheet, but it is recommended that you use one that is relatively simple and doesn't contain a lot of small text.

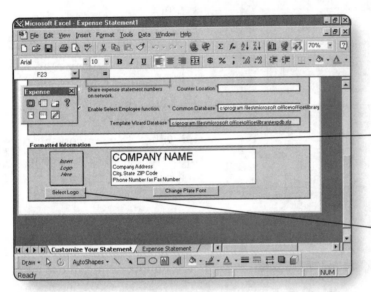

1. **Scroll down** to the **Formatted Information area** on the Customize Your Statement worksheet.

2. **Click** on the **Select Logo button**. The Insert Picture dialog box will be displayed.

3. **Locate** the **image file** you want to use as a logo.

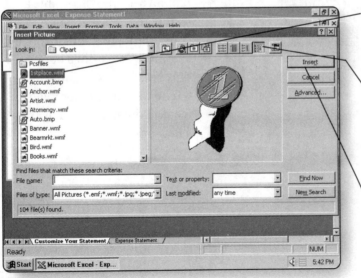

4. **Click** on the **file**. It will be highlighted.

TIP

To preview a picture in the Insert Picture dialog box, click on the Preview button.

5. **Click** on **Insert**. The Insert Picture dialog box will close.

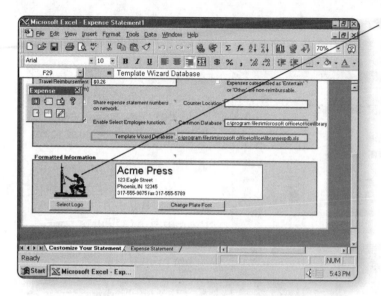

Excel will insert the picture you specified into the logo area on the Customize Your Statement worksheet. Notice that Excel automatically resizes the image to fit in the space allotted for the logo.

Changing Worksheet Fonts

You can change the plate font used on your Expense Statement worksheet. The plate font refers to the font used for the Expense Statement worksheet "boilerplate" text. This is the text that appears at the top of the worksheet.

1. **Click** on the **Change Plate Font button**. The Format Cells dialog box will open.

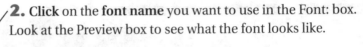

2. **Click** on the **font name** you want to use in the Font: box. Look at the Preview box to see what the font looks like.

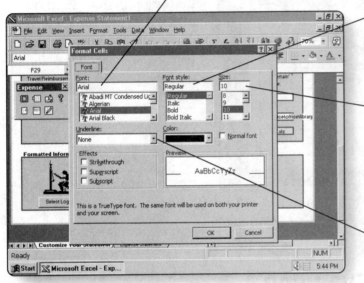

3. **Click** on the **style** you want to assign to the font in the Font style: box. You can choose Regular, Italic, Bold, and so on.

4. **Click** on the **font size** you want to assign to the font in the Size: box. You don't want to set the font size to high or your worksheet will become crowded or not print correctly.

5. **Click** on the **down arrow** (▼) for the Underline: box. A drop-down list will appear.

6. **Click** on the **type** of **underlining** you want to assign to the font. By default, the None option is selected.

7. **Click** on the **down arrow** (▼) for the Color box. A drop-down list will appear.

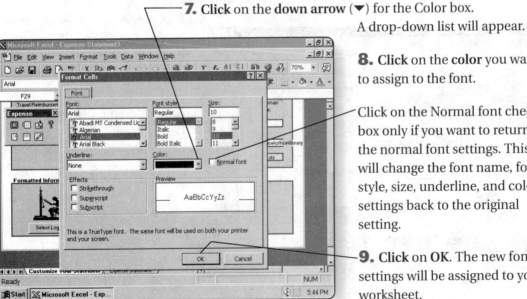

8. **Click** on the **color** you want to assign to the font.

Click on the Normal font check box only if you want to return to the normal font settings. This will change the font name, font style, size, underline, and color settings back to the original setting.

9. **Click** on **OK**. The new font settings will be assigned to your worksheet.

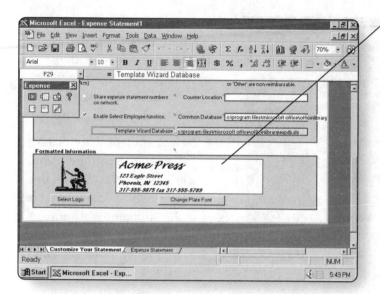

You can see an example of the font and options you selected by looking at the sample text window above the Change Plate Font button on the Customize Your Statement worksheet.

USING THE EXPENSE TOOLBAR

You've probably noticed the small Expense toolbar floating on your screen. This toolbar appears when you first display the Customize Your Statement worksheet. The Expense toolbar provides a few commands to help you use the Customize Your Statement worksheet:

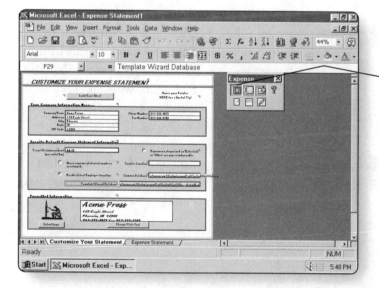

✦ **Size to Screen/Return to Size button.** Click on this button to reduce the view of the worksheet so you can see the full worksheet on your screen. Click it again to return to Normal view.

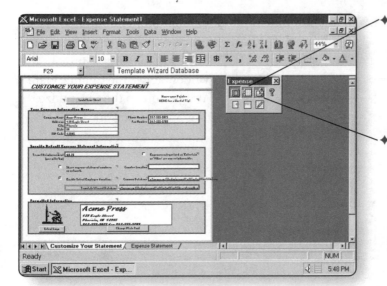

✦ **Hide Comments/Display Comments.** Click on this button once to hide the comment triangles on the worksheet; click on it again to display the comment triangles.

✦ **New Comment.** This enables you to enter a comment about a cell. When you click on this button, a blank comment box with your name will appear next to the selected cell. Enter a comment for that cell and then click someplace else on the worksheet to save your comment with the worksheet.

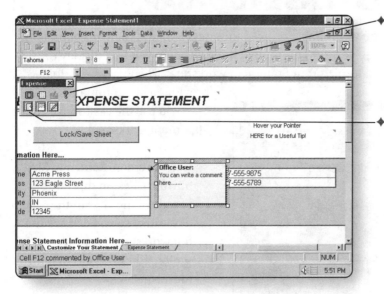

✦ **Template Help.** By clicking on this button a window with help on how to use the Expense Statement template will be displayed.

✦ **Display Example/Remove Example.** Click on this button and then click on the Expense Statement worksheet tab to see example data. Click on this button again to remove the example and click on the Customize button to return to the Customize Your Statement worksheet.

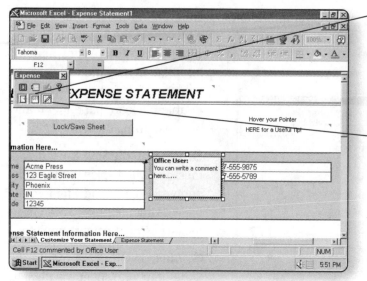

✦ **Assign a Number.** Click on this button if you want Excel to insert a sequential number for each time you use the Expense Statement worksheet.

✦ **Capture Data in a Database.** Click on this button if you have a database set up to store information you enter on the Expense Statement worksheet.

LOCKING AND SAVING YOUR NEW TEMPLATE

After you customize the Customize Your Statement worksheet, you need to save and lock those settings. When you lock the worksheet, this ensures that your customized settings do not change.

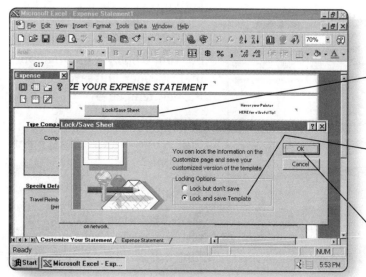

1. **Click** on the **Lock/Save Sheet button.** The Lock/Save Sheet dialog box will open.

2. **Click** on **Lock and save Template** in the Locking Options box. The option will be selected.

3. **Click** on **OK.** The Save Template dialog box will open.

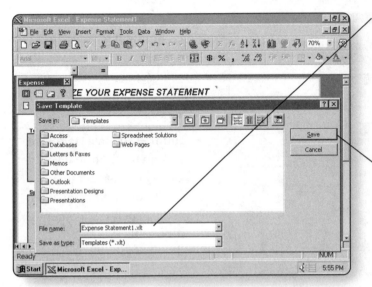

4. Type a **name** for the new template in the File name: text box. If you want save the new template in the Spreadsheet Solutions folder, be sure to double-click on that folder name before naming the file.

5. **Click** on the **Save button**. A message will display letting you know where your new template file is stored. It also tells you how to start using the new template.

6. **Click** on **OK**. The Expense Statement worksheet will display.

FINISHING YOUR EXPENSE STATEMENT

You still are working in the template file, so any changes you make to the expense statement will be saved with that template. Notice in the Employee section that you do not have anything currently entered. If you are the only one who will use this expense statement, you can fill out your employee information in this section and save it with the new template.

1. **Click** in the **cell** next to the text "Name." The insertion point will appear.

2. Type your **name**.

3. **Repeat steps 1** and **2** for the rest of the cells (SSN, Department, Emp #, Position, Manager, and Fax Number) in the Employee box.

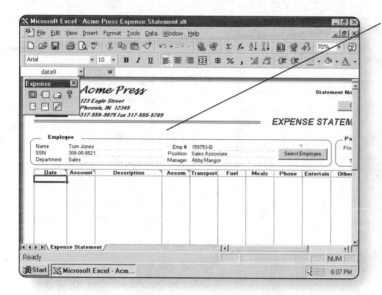

Here's an example of how the Employee section looks with the customized data inserted.

TIP

Look around the rest of the worksheet to see if there are any other areas you might customize. One area you might want to customize or delete is at the bottom of the worksheet, where it says "Insert Fine Print Here."

SAVING FINAL CUSTOMIZATION SETTINGS

After you make final changes to the Expense Statement worksheet template, you must save the template again.

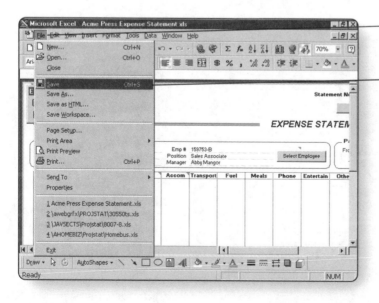

1. Click on File. The File menu will appear.

2. Click on Save. Excel will display the Template File – Save to Database dialog box. This dialog box informs you that you need to save the employee information.

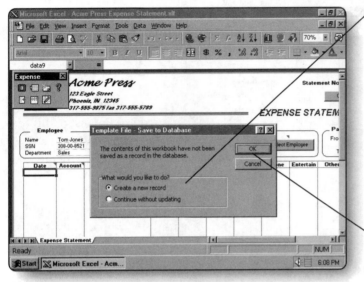

3. **Choose** one of the following options:

✦ **Create a new record.** If you have a database that stores employee information, click on this option.

✦ **Continue without updating.** If you do not use a database with the Expense Statement template, click on this option.

4. **Click** on **OK**. The dialog box will close. Now you can open a new file based on this template and enter actual expense data.

Glossary

+. Addition operator.

-. Subtraction operator.

=. Initiates all formulas.

*. Multiplication operator.

/. Division operator.

>. Greater than operator.

<. Less than operator.

<>. Not equal to operator.

:. Range operator.

A

Absolute reference. References to cell addresses that don't change based on where a formula is located in a worksheet.

Active cell. The selected cell in a worksheet.

Address. A named reference to a cell based on its location at the intersection of a column and row; for example, the cell in the fourth row of the second column has an address of B4.

Alignment. The arrangement of text or an object in relation to the document's margins in Word, a slide's dimensions in PowerPoint, or a cell's edges in Excel. Alignment can be left, right, centered, or justified.

Array. A contiguous set of cells in a worksheet.

AutoFormat. Pre-defined sets of styles that allow you to quickly apply formatting (color, font, etc.) to your Excel worksheet.

AutoSum. A built-in addition function that allows you to add a row or column of figures using the AutoSum button on the Excel toolbar.

Axis (pl. axes). In a graph, one of two value sets (*see also* y-axis and x-axis).

B

Bar chart. A type of chart that uses bars of varying lengths to represent values.

Border. A formatting option that places a line around any of the four sides of an object, such as a cell.

C

Cell. The area defined by a rectangle at which a row and column intersect in an Excel worksheet.

Cell Reference. A method of referring to a cell in a formula by listing the location of its row and column intersection.

Chart. Also called *graph*. A chart is a visual representation of numerical data.

Circular Reference. In a formula, a circular reference indicates that a calculation should return to its starting point and repeat endlessly; a circular reference in a formula will result in an error message.

Clip art. Ready-made line drawings that are included with Office in the Clip Art Gallery; these drawings can be inserted into Office documents.

Column. A set of cells running vertically down a worksheet.

Combination chart. A chart that uses more than one style of representing data; for example, bars for one set of data and a line for another set of data. A chart that shows rainfall in a country by month with bars and the average rainfall in the world with a line is an example of a combination chart.

D

Data. Information, which can be either numerical or textual.

Data series. In charts, elements that represent a set of data, such as pie segment, line, or bar.

Data type. The category of numerical data, such as currency, scientific, or percentage.

Desktop. Windows' main work area.

Drag-and-drop. A feature that allows you to move an object or selected text around an Excel worksheet using your mouse.

E

Equation. *See* formula.

F

Fill. A function that allows Excel to automatically complete a series of numbers based on an established pattern.

Fill (color). A formatting feature used to apply color or a pattern to the interior of an object, such as a cell.

Fill Handle. A block at the bottom right corner of all cells in a worksheet that is used to fill cells as it is dragged across with a pattern of data.

Filter. To make settings so that only cells that meet certain criteria are displayed in your worksheet.

Financial functions. Functions (stored formulas) that are used with money, such as payments and interest rates.

Flip. To turn an object on a page 180 degrees.

Font. A design family of text, also called a *typeface*.

Footer. Text repeated at the bottom of each page of a document.

Format. To apply settings for font, color, size, and style to data or objects.

Formula. An equation that instructs Excel to perform certain calculations based on numerical data in designated cells.

Formula bar. The location where all data and formulas are entered for a selected cell.

Freezing. In large worksheets it is sometimes desirable to freeze a portion of the sheet, such as column headings, so that it doesn't scroll off screen when you move down the page.

Function. A pre-defined, named formula.

G

General format. A numerical type applied to numbers in cells.

Goal Seek. A feature that allows you to enter the result you want. Excel then determines changes in the formula or data required to obtain the result.

Go To. A feature of Excel that allows you to move quickly to a page or cell of your worksheet based on criteria you provide.

Graphs. *See* charts.

Greater than. A function that restricts a number result to be higher than a named number.

Gridlines. Lines between the cells of a worksheet which can be displayed and printed or not.

H

Header. Text repeated at the top of each page of a document.

Hide. A feature of Excel that allows you to temporarily stop displaying designated cells in a worksheet.

I

Icon. In software, a picture representing a feature, such as tool button icon.

IF function. A pre-defined formula indicating that a result is to occur only if some criteria is met. For example, you could use this function to indicate that "if the result of a sum is greater than 10, the result should appear in this cell."

J

Justify. To space a line of text across a cell evenly from the left margin to the right margin.

L

Label. A descriptive text element added to a chart to help the reader understand a visual element. Also refers to row or column headings.

Landscape. A page orientation that prints a document with the long edge of the paper across the top.

Legend. A definition of the various elements of a chart or graph.

Less than. A pre-defined function that indicates a result should occur only if a number is less than the specified number.

Logical functions. Functions that are based on the logical consequence of a named set of circumstances, such as the IF . . . THEN function.

M

Macro. A saved series of keystrokes that can be played back to perform an action.

Maps. Representing data in charts with geographical maps rather than traditional chart elements such as bars and lines.

Mathematical functions. Functions that produce mathematical results, such as SUM and AVG.

N

Name definitions. Providing an alternate name for a cell so you can use that name definition in formulas.

Named ranges. Providing a name for a set of cells so you can use that name in formulas.

O

Object. A picture, map, or other graphic element that you can place in an Excel worksheet.

Office Assistant. A help feature for Microsoft Office products that allows you to ask questions in standard English sentence format.

Operator. The parts of a formula that indicate an action to be performed, such as addition (+) or division (/).

Optional arguments. A portion of a formula which is not necessary to achieve the result, but that designates an action other than the default. An optional argument to include decimals in a result would include the decimal point and two zeros even if the number doesn't contain cents.

Orientation. The way a document prints on a piece of paper; landscape prints with the longer side of a page on top, while portrait prints with the shorter edge at the top.

P

Passwords. A word selected by an Excel user to protect a worksheet; once a sheet is protected, the correct password must be entered to modify that sheet.

Paste. To place an object or text placed on the Windows clipboard in a document.

Patterns. Pre-defined shading and line arrangements used to format cells in a worksheet.

Pie chart. A round chart type in which each pie wedge represents a value.

Plot. The area of a chart where data is drawn using elements such as line, bars, or pie wedges.

Portrait. A page orientation where a document prints with the shorter edge of the paper along the top.

Precedent. Some formulas call on data that is the result of another formula; the precedent is the formula that originally created the data being named in the second formula.

Print area. The portion of a worksheet you designate to print.

Print Preview. A feature that allows you to view a document on your screen appearing as it will when printed.

Protection. To make settings to a worksheet so that only those authorized can modify the worksheet.

R

Range. A collection of cells, ranging from the first named cell to the last.

Recalculation. Used with manual calculation, recalculation is applied to a formula when data has changed to receive the new result.

Redo. A feature of Excel that allows you to repeat an action you have reversed using the Undo feature.

Reference. In a formula, a name or range that refers the formula to a cell or set of cells.

Relative. In a formula, making reference to a cell relative to the location of the cell where the formula is placed; if the formula cell is moved, the cell being referenced changes in relation to the new location.

Rotate. To manipulate an object so that it moves around a 360 degree axis.

Row. A set of cells running from left to right across a worksheet.

S

Save as. To save a previously saved worksheet with a new name or properties.

Scroll bar. A device used to move up and down or left to right in a worksheet to display various portions of it onscreen.

Shading. A gray to black pattern used to format cells in a worksheet.

Sheet. *See* Worksheet.

Solver. A feature that helps you locate the appropriate formula to achieve a specific result.

Sort. To arrange information in a column or row alphanumerically, in ascending or descending order.

Spelling. A feature of Excel that verifies the spelling of words in your worksheets.

Spreadsheet. A software program used to perform calculations on data.

Style. A saved, named set of formatting such as color, size, and font that can be applied to data in a worksheet.

SUM function. A saved, named function of addition that can be applied to cells by typing the term "SUM" in a formula.

Syntax. The structure and order of the functions and references used in a formula.

T

Target cell. The cell where the results of a formula should be placed.

Template. A pre-defined set of worksheet formats included with Excel that are useful for quickly generating certain types of documents, such as an invoice.

Text box. A text object that you can create with the drawing feature of Excel to place text anywhere on a chart or worksheet; often used to label elements of a chart or worksheet.

Titles. Names of the elements of a chart.

Trendline. A line that can be overlaid on a chart to indicate a trend from the data in the chart.

U

Undo. An Excel feature that allows you to reverse the last action performed.

Unhide. To reveal cells previously hidden in a worksheet.

Unprotect. To remove password safeguards from a worksheet so that anyone can modify the worksheet.

V

Value. Value is another term for a number.

Variable. Cells that are changed to see what results from that change.

W

What if. A scenario in a formula that supposes certain criteria.

What's This?. A part of the Excel Help system; once you select What's This? your cursor changes to a question mark and you can click on any on-screen element to receive an explanation of that element.

Wizard. A feature of Excel that walks you through a procedure step by step; a wizard creates something, such as a chart, using the answers you give to a series of questions.

Wrapping. A function that causes text to automatically wrap to the next line when it reaches the right edge of a cell.

Workbook. A single Excel file containing a collection of Excel worksheets.

Worksheet. One of several pages in an Excel workbook.

X

X-axis. In a chart, the vertical-value axis.

y

Y-axis. In a chart, the horizontal-value axis.

Index

PPMT (Principal Payment) function, 254–255

principal, calculating for amortization table, 254–255

principal payment (PPMT) function, 254–255

Print button, 23

printing

    color *vs.* black and white, 147

    comments, 147

    multiple copies, 23–24

    Page Setup options, 142, 147

        headers and footers, 144–146

        margins, 143–144

        paper size, 142–143

        portrait *vs.* landscape, 142

        print quality, 142

        selecting rows and columns, 146–148

    setting Print Area, 148

    viewing worksheet before, 149–152

    worksheet, 153

        partial, 23–24, 148

Protect Sheet, 115

Protect Workbook, 118

R

range

    filling, 49–51

    moving directly to, 84–85

    naming, 82–83

    selecting, 40

"Ready" indicator, 16

recording macros, 96–98

Redo button, 44

#REF! error message, 79

relative cell references, 69

Replace command, 87–88

review questions

    Part I, 36

    Part II, 154

    Part III, 192

    Part IV, 228

    Part V, 275

    Part VI, 298

rotating text, 164

rows

    adding, 42–43, 268–269

    adjusting height, 53–54

    converting to columns, 51–53

    deleting, 42

    freezing labels, 93–94

    hiding, 89–90

        displaying hidden, 90–91

    moving or copying, 45–49

    selecting for printing, 146–148

    sorting, 106–108

running macros, 99–100

S

Save As, 22, 120

saving

    files, 22, 25

    templates, 134–136, 138–139

    worksheets, 33

scenarios, 115

scroll bars, 16

Scroll lock, 16

search engine, 287

searching worksheet, 111–114

series, labeling, 207

shadow, adding to charts, 210

sheet. *See* worksheet